DOING QUALITATIV
DESK-BASED RESEAF

A Practical Guide to Writing
an Excellent Dissertation

Barbara Bassot

First published in Great Britain in 2022 by

Policy Press, an imprint of
Bristol University Press
University of Bristol
1-9 Old Park Hill
Bristol
BS2 8BB
UK
+44 (0)117 954 5940
bup-info@bristol.ac.uk

Details of international sales and distribution partners are available at
policy.bristoluniversitypress.co.uk

British Library Cataloguing in Publication Data
A catalogue record for this book is available from the British Library

ISBN 978-1-4473-6243-2 paperback
ISBN 978-1-4473-6244-9 ePub
ISBN 978-1-4473-6245-6 ePDF

Cover design: Nicky Borowiec
Front cover image: Adobe Stock/svetlaborovko

Bristol University Press and Policy Press use environmentally responsible
print partners

Printed and bound in Great Britain by CMP, Poole

Contents

Contents

List of figures and tables

Figures

Tables

Glossary

anonymity	ensuring that research participants cannot be identified
assumptions	things we take for granted and no longer think about
autonomy	being free to make decisions for yourself without pressure or influence
bias	reaching inaccurate conclusions based on little information or evidence
confidentiality	keeping information that participants disclose private
content analysis	identifying how many times things are said or written
copyright	the legal right of an individual to maintain their intellectual property
critical reflection	more personal than criticality and includes being aware of our strengths and weaknesses, understanding how we think and learn
criticality	taking a questioning approach to everything
curiosity	wanting to know and understand more
deductive reasoning	moving from big to small, more commonly used in quantitative research
desk-based research	a form of empirical research where you gather your data indirectly (for example, via the internet)
discourse analysis	analysing how things are said and what is not said because it has been implied, omitted or ignored
empirical research	research where you gather your own data directly from participants
epistemology	how we know what we know

ethics	a branch of philosophy that deals with morals and acts as a guide regarding how people are meant to behave
evaluation	exploring and assessing the value and effectiveness of something
flow chart	a diagram showing a process or flow of work
Gantt chart	a visual view of tasks scheduled over time
generalisability	findings from a research study that can be applied in similar circumstances or situations to wider populations
hypothesis	a proposed explanation based on what you think you will find and a focus for further exploration – usually applies to quantitative research
inductive reasoning	moving from small to big – more commonly used in qualitative research
informed consent	permission given freely by research participants with an understanding of what the study and their participation involves
interpretivism	examines non-numerical data in order to interpret it and gain new insights, and underpins qualitative research in the social sciences
library-based research	another term for secondary research
method	quantitative or qualitative
methodology	a system that uses theory to explain a set of broad principles or rules governing how a piece of research is carried out
methods	techniques used to carry out research, for example, interviews, questionnaires, observations
mind maps	diagrams showing the links between aspects of a topic or issue

narrative analysis   analysing the story being told

non–maleficence   do no harm

objectivism   an approach to research based on fact

ontology   the view of reality adopted in research

positionality   being clear about your position in relation to your research, including any assumptions you might be making and any preconceived ideas about your topic you might have

positivism   using scientific enquiry in order to provide answers to questions or solutions to problems, and underpins quantitative research in the social sciences

primary sources   original material, which includes academic journal articles that publish findings from primary research

qualitative   research exploring non-numerical data to gain insights

quantitative   research that uses numerical data to test a hypothesis

reflexivity   a high level of self-awareness in relation to our pre-existing thoughts on a topic or area and being ready to challenge them

reliability   being able to repeat a piece of research in similar circumstances and get largely the same results

research   systematic investigation or inquiry into a topic or area

research proposal   a document showing what you are proposing to research and how you intend to do this

research question   something to explore and open to multiple answers – usually applies to qualitative research

research, secondary   research that uses the data from previous studies to gain new insights and interpretations in relation to a new research question

secondary sources sources that describe or analyse primary sources, including textbooks, dictionaries, encyclopaedias and other written material that review and evaluate original sources

subjectivism an approach to research based on the researcher's interpretation

tertiary sources sources that compile and organise mostly (although not exclusively) secondary sources to make them easier to find, including catalogues and databases

thematic analysis the most common technique for analysing qualitative data – involves identifying words and phrases that seem particularly significant in relation to your research question and grouping them

theory an individual's (or two people's, or even a group of people's) explanation of a particular phenomenon, based on research

thick descriptions give a sense of what it is like to experience that setting or group from the standpoint of the people experiencing it

transferability providing sufficient evidence in qualitative research to show that the findings could be applied to other situations

triangulation examining something from more than one viewpoint

trustworthiness writing thick descriptions of how qualitative research has been carried out and how the data has been analysed and interpreted that shows a study can be trusted

validity measuring what you set out to measure

Virtual Learning Environment (VLE) a web-based platform for the digital aspects of a course of study

Acknowledgements

I would like to express my sincere thanks to my family and friends for all their support in the process of bringing this book into fruition. In particular, I would like to thank Martin Bassot for his excellent work on the diagrams and Marc Bassot for his proofreading and constructive comments. I would also like to thank the reviewers of the proposal and typescript whose positive, constructive and helpful comments helped me to develop the work into the book it has become. I would especially like to thank my commissioning editor, Catherine Gray, for her support, friendship and invaluable advice which she provided at every step along the way, from the initial idea shared in a coffee shop to its publication. I would also like to thank the publisher for being ready to publish a different, but much-needed, research methods book that I believe will support many students with their qualitative desk-based projects.

How to use this book

This book is a step-by-step guide to doing a qualitative desk-based research project and as such it is different from many research methods textbooks. This is because the majority of research methods books focus primarily on empirical research where data is collected from participants directly – for example, through interviews, focus groups or questionnaires – and there is usually only a small amount of content on research projects that are desk-based. By contrast, this book focuses completely on research where the data used is already available, often via the internet, ready to be identified, collected and analysed.

Students can undertake a desk-based study for a variety of reasons. For example, it could be because it has proved difficult, even impossible, to collect data in more traditional ways, or because they discovered that desk-based research could open up interesting new insights into their chosen subject. Doing a desk-based project has enabled many students to complete dissertations successfully, imaginatively and on subjects that have been of considerable personal interest.

The overall aim of the book is twofold. First, it will take you through the process of carrying out a qualitative piece of desk-based research one step at a time from start to finish. As it is designed to be practical, it is written sequentially from starting a project right through to its completion. Second, my hope is to enable you to fulfil the ultimate goal of producing a dissertation you can be proud of. An independent research project is a fantastic opportunity not only to demonstrate your academic knowledge but also to prove your skills in working independently. I hope the guidance in this book will give you the confidence to carry it off to the best of your ability.

Research methods books can often seem rather dry, which is a shame when your dissertation could well be one of the most motivational pieces of work you will engage in as a student. I've chosen three case studies of students in the final year of their degree to bring what can feel like a messy and challenging process to life. Although fictitious, their stories are inspired by students I have known and I hope they will help you see not only the rich potential of desk-based research but also the different ways in which students overcome the challenges of the research process. Sam, Rajesh and Emma are all doing desk-based projects on different topics and all of them are studying for degrees where a desk-based study is giving them an excellent way of researching a topic that might be difficult otherwise:

- Sam (short for Samantha or Samuel) is really interested in the experiences of refugees and has been for a very long time. Sam's mum was a refugee and Sam really wants to understand more of what she went through and to learn more about people with a refugee heritage.

- Rajesh has always loved music. Growing up he played various musical instruments and now plays drums in a band. He also plays percussion in the university orchestra. Since studying at university he has become interested in the impact of music on mental health and wellbeing.
- Emma is doing her research project on what makes people offend and reoffend. This links to some career ideas she has for the future and reflects the passion for equality and social justice that she has developed during her degree course.

I have also used two conceptual tools to help you along the way; both were developed during my teaching of research methods. The first is the Metaphorical Tent and this is used throughout the book to symbolise the key elements you will need to grapple with in order to turn your research project into a dissertation. The second is the Research Triangle and this depicts the ongoing process of analysing and reviewing the literature and the data which underpins every piece of qualitative research.

In addition, you will see a number of icons used in the book as visual prompts, as follows:

 Key points highlight important content as succinctly as possible, so that it's easy to grasp and find again if you need to.

 Top tips offer snippets of practical advice that are again the product of teaching.

 Pitfalls capture some of the traps students can fall into and which you'll want to avoid.

 Talk to your supervisor is a reminder to seek support and advice when you need it.

 Write in your research journal encourages you to capture your thinking process.

All of these can help you to turn a good dissertation into an excellent piece of work.

In addition, there is a glossary of key terms at the start of the book for ease of reference and each time a term is used for the first time in the text it is highlighted in bold.

Each chapter finishes with a short list for further reading with commentary, so that you have some ideas of where you could go next when you feel you need to learn more. There is also a full list of references at the back of the book to enable you to follow up on any sources of interest.

The book is organised into three parts. Part I, 'Preparing the ground', focuses on the early work you need to do to prepare for your research project. Part II,

'Assembling the structure', examines each element of the research process as you start putting your project together. Part III, 'Keeping your tent stable and secure', explores the important aspects of getting the support you need and managing the project as a whole.

Qualitative research cannot necessarily be carried out in a linear fashion, and I have written this book so that you can use it flexibly. Reading the book from cover to cover before starting a project or as part of a research methods module could give you a very useful overview of what you need to do. However, I am expecting this to be a book that you will dip in and out of at various points during your project, so don't be afraid to find your own path through it. The sub-headings in the table of contents will give you a good indication of where to find different areas of discussion and the index will take you to specific passages relating to key ideas. In particular, you might want to read the chapters in Part III in the early days of your research process as they give some important tips to help you to manage your project effectively while taking advantage of the support that is available.

The book's content is arranged in the following way. In Part I, Chapter 1 gives an introduction to some key terms related to qualitative desk-based research and the concepts of the Metaphorical Tent and the Research Triangle are explained. Chapter 2 focuses on choosing a topic; this is absolutely essential for you to get started. Chapter 3 examines the importance of keeping a research journal. It is very helpful to start doing this in the early stages of your project as it can save you lots of valuable time later on. Chapter 4 takes you through the process of completing a research proposal. This is often a key element of a research methods module and is an important document if you need to gain ethical clearance from your university.

Part II starts with Chapter 5 and covers the vital area of your research question that keeps your Metaphorical Tent upright and stable. This is something you will return to and revisit as you engage with the Research Triangle. Chapter 6 emphasises the importance of considering the background and context for your research, which will form an important part of the introduction to your dissertation. Chapter 7 is a pivotal chapter in the whole book and helps you to consider what you will use as your data. Many research methods books contain very little on finding and using data indirectly, for example, via the internet. Your decision on your choice of data will be vital in ensuring the success of your study and will need to be made in the light of some robust criteria. Chapter 8 focuses on the literature review and Chapter 9 examines a range of desk-based methodologies. Chapter 10 critically evaluates a range of ethical issues relevant to desk-based research and in Chapter 11 we move on to techniques for data analysis. Part II finishes with Chapter 12 and focuses on writing conclusions and recommendations.

Part III contains lots of useful information to help you with your project overall and starts with Chapter 13, which identifies the different ways you can get the support you need to help you complete a successful research project. The final chapter considers various aspects of managing your project well. Both of the chapters in Part III are ones that you may well want to read early in the process of doing your research and you are likely to want to revisit them at various points along the way.

Good luck with your studies!

PART I

Preparing the ground

In Part I we focus on making sure that the ground is well prepared for erecting your Metaphorical Tent. This includes learning more about the tent itself and the advantages and disadvantages of **desk-based research**. We then move on to choosing a topic, keeping a research journal and the nuts and bolts of writing a **research proposal**. All of this is part of making sure that you are in a strong position to start your desk-based research project. We see how Sam, Rajesh and Emma get on in the early stages of their research projects.

1

Introduction

In this chapter we will:

- ☐ underline the importance of a dissertation;

- ☐ explain the scope and some of the terminology used in the book;

- ☐ discuss the term **qualitative** research;

- ☐ explain the different kinds of data sources that are available;

- ☐ explain the term desk-based research and discuss its advantages and disadvantages;

- ☐ learn about the Metaphorical Tent and the Research Triangle.

You are probably reading this book because you are planning, beginning or actually in the process of undertaking a small piece of qualitative research, which will lead to you writing a dissertation. You might be studying a research methods module in preparation for your project or doing the project itself. You are likely to be in the latter stages of your undergraduate degree, although some of you reading this book might be postgraduates who are new to this whole area because you didn't write a dissertation as part of your first degree. This book is designed as a practical guide to help you progress along each step of the way towards this.

The specific focus of this book is on qualitative desk-based research. Many students in the social sciences (and in some other academic disciplines, such as humanities and business studies) and those on professional courses (for example, social work, counselling and youth work) want to undertake qualitative research, but they might not feel comfortable with, or be able to, talk to people and gather data directly for a number of valid reasons. In such cases, what is termed an **empirical** study is often not possible on ethical and practical grounds, so using other sources of data is necessary. This data can take many different forms and this book will show how you can write a vibrant and engaging dissertation that is solidly grounded in relevant **theory** and its application, without being in direct contact with research participants. In many ways, desk-based research is what it says it is – research that you can do without leaving your desk, but definitely without being chained to it!

EMPIRICAL – research where you gather your own data (for example, through interviews, focus groups).

DESK-BASED – a form of empirical research where you gather your data indirectly (for example, via the internet).

There are a large number of books on the whole area of research methods that seek to carefully consider and explain the many different concepts and tools that you need to understand in order to carry out a research project well. These can be categorised into three main groups:

1. Books that focus on the process of doing a research project – examples here are *The Good Research Guide* (Denscombe, 2017), *How to Do Your Research Project* (Thomas, 2017) and *Doing Your Research Project* (Bell and Waters, 2018). Many of my own students use one or more of these as their 'go-to' books on research methods.
2. Larger textbooks that focus on explaining and exploring terminology and key concepts in research – examples here are *Social Research Methods* (Bryman, 2016), *Research Methods in Education* (Cohen et al, 2018) and *The Sage Handbook of Qualitative Research* (Denzin and Lincoln, 2018). Students often use these to gain a deeper understanding of research terminology and are most likely to read specific chapters rather than the whole book.
3. Books that are discipline-specific – examples include *An Introduction to Research Methods in Education* (Punch and Oancea, 2014), *Research Methods and Statistics in Psychology* (Coolican, 2018), *Making Sense of Research in Nursing, Health and Social Care* (Moule, 2018) and *Research Methods for Business Students* (Saunders et al, 2019).

You will want to become familiar with a number of these and always be sure to follow the recommendations of your research methods tutors. Remember, overall, there are far too many research methods books for you to be able to read them all and often they will be books that you dip in and out of. A number of research methods texts will be referred to throughout this book and at the end of each chapter you will find some recommendations for further reading. In addition, at the back of the book you will find a full list of references to guide you to everything easily in your library. As well as books on research methods, there are those that focus on the process of writing a good dissertation. These will also be referred to and are included in the reference list.

Being proud of your dissertation

Writing a dissertation is a large and often somewhat daunting task, especially when you are doing it for the first time. It is no mean feat and often comes when there are many other pressures to cope with, such as examinations to revise for, placements to complete, postgraduate courses to consider, and at a time when graduate schemes and other jobs with complex application processes with tight deadlines loom large. This all happens when you will be preparing for your next major transition from university to whatever comes next (Adams et al, 1976; Bridges, 2004).

However, many students look forward to doing their dissertation as it gives them the time and scope to delve more deeply into an area they are interested in. Often it gives students the opportunity to really get their teeth into something they are passionate about, and it could help prepare them for a future career. Most dissertations attract a larger number of credits than a single module and, as a result, they can often feel that they have a lot riding on them, not least of which is your overall degree classification. Producing a high-quality dissertation involves a lot of work; hence many students feel it really matters.

Scope and terminology

Many of my own students find some of the terminology used in research difficult to understand and in general this is because it is abstract. In addition, tutors and writers in this area do not always agree with one another when it comes to definitions, which can make things very confusing. When writing this book, I made some key decisions in relation to the scope and terminology used; for clarity here is a summary.

First, in relation to the scope of the book, academic staff in the social sciences regularly discuss the content for research methods modules to ensure it is appropriate. Such modules are commonly studied at undergraduate and postgraduate level. Some academics (but not all) agree that undergraduate students should be able to show some grasp of **methodology** at a philosophical level. This will often be demonstrated through a discussion of the key research paradigms of **positivism** and **interpretivism**. Other academics argue that at this level an understanding of the difference between **quantitative** and qualitative research is sufficient. The latter mirrors the approach taken by writers such as Greetham (2019) and Cottrell (2014) as shown by the content of their publications. All academics rightly argue that postgraduate students need to show more understanding than undergraduates, including a grasp of areas like constructivism, critical theory, ethnography, grounded theory, narrative, phenomenology and case study – as the content of Biggam's (2018) text demonstrates. Some argue that this is appropriate at undergraduate level too. The approach taken in this book is that having a grasp of the philosophical positions of positivism and interpretivism and the differences between quantitative and qualitative research will equip you well for your studies. I have tried to make this challenging area as accessible as I can to make it understandable, but without dumbing it down. But, if your particular research methods module also includes other philosophical aspects as discussed, and if you are studying at postgraduate level, you will need to read additional recommended literature on these.

Second, some research terminology is potentially confusing, and this applies particularly to the terms **method** and **methods**, which are often used interchangeably in published literature. For the purpose of clarity in this book, they are used in the following way. The term method (in the singular) refers to the choice of approach – quantitative or qualitative; the focus here is on qualitative method. The term methods (in the plural) refers to the specific techniques that researchers use to carry out their studies, such as questionnaires, interviews and observations.

A decision was also made not to use two particular terms. First, the term research objectives: this usually means the specific things that someone is trying to achieve (or even answers they are trying to find) through their study. The view taken here is that this term is best used in quantitative studies. In this book the term **research question** is preferred because qualitative research often involves gaining insights and understandings rather than specific outputs. Second, the term research strategy has also not been used. This is an umbrella term that encompasses each of the planned aspects of your study, and the focus of this book is on each particular aspect of it rather than the whole.

SAM

Hi, my name is Sam and I'm in the final year of my degree course. I'm really interested in the experiences of refugees; it feels like I've been interested in this area for as long as I can remember – my whole life really. Mum was a refugee and has told me so many amazing stories as I was growing up. She obviously went through such a lot and it's made me really want to learn more about people with a refugee heritage so I can understand more of what she went through.

What is qualitative research?

Defining the term qualitative research is not particularly straightforward, but one simple way of doing this is to say that it is any kind of research that doesn't involve numbers. As Punch and Oancea (2014: 3) state, 'Qualitative research is empirical research where the data are not in the form of numbers.' But such a definition only tells us what qualitative research isn't, and not what it is. In general, qualitative research involves exploring things in order to gain understandings via interpretation. As Denzin and Lincoln (2018: 10) explain succinctly, 'qualitative researchers study things in their natural settings, attempting to make sense of, or interpret phenomena in terms of the meanings people bring to them'.

Qualitative research involves exploring data and interpreting phenomena to gain insights rather than to get answers or solutions.

At this point, it is useful to note the relatively unusual use of plurals in relation to the words understanding and meaning. In qualitative research it is accepted that people experience things differently and hence, do not see the world in the same way. The word interpretivist is usually associated with qualitative research and because people (including researchers) also see things differently, there will always be more than one interpretation leading to more than one understanding and more than one meaning, hence the use of plurals.

Meanings and understandings (both plural) are great words to include in a qualitative dissertation.

Most commonly the data gathered by qualitative researchers is verbal, using methods such as interviews and focus groups. However, as this book shows, you can do this in a number of other ways, especially when direct access to participants in their natural settings is difficult, or even impossible, for a range of reasons.

What is desk-based research?

Many students who want to carry out a qualitative study face the question, 'How can I do qualitative research when I can't talk to the relevant people?' One response to this question might be provided by doing a desk-based project. So, what is desk-based research and what does it involve?

The term desk-based research covers a wide range of ways in which you can carry out a robust study by gathering qualitative data from existing sources. In general, there are three different types of data sources that are used in the process of carrying out a research project: **primary sources**, **secondary sources** and **tertiary sources**. These are explained next.

Primary data sources contain material that is original. This kind of material is often written, and examples are poems, diaries and historical records. But they can also be visual, such as paintings, photographs and diagrams as well as things that have been recorded via audio or visual media like podcasts, documentaries and films.

Secondary data sources describe or analyse primary sources. These include textbooks, dictionaries, encyclopaedias and other written material that review and evaluate original sources. These reviews might also be done by audio or visual means, such as via radio, TV programmes, blogs and video logs (vlogs). Secondary sources also include academic journal articles that publish findings from primary research.

Tertiary data sources compile and organise mostly (although not exclusively) secondary sources to make them easier to find. These offer a key guide, especially at the beginning of a project, and include catalogues (such as the one for your university library), databases (like EBSCO and ProQuest) which can guide you to relevant academic journal articles, and those that particularly focus on finding abstracts (such as Educational Abstracts Online).

You will probably use all of these sources at some point in the process of carrying out a desk-based study, but you are likely to draw the data for your study from primary sources. This will be discussed in much more detail in Chapter 7.

At this point it is important to explain the terms desk-based research, **secondary research** and **library-based research**. These three terms are sometimes used interchangeably, which again can be confusing because they do not necessarily mean exactly the same thing. For the purpose of this book, the term desk-based research is defined as research where you gather your own data indirectly (for example, via the internet) in order to examine and interpret it in relation to relevant theory. This means it is a form of primary research because you collect your own data. By contrast, secondary research involves using the data collected by others (often as part of published research studies) and interpreting that data to gain new insights in relation to your research question. This often involves examining a number of studies in a given area in order to reach some conclusions that were not part of the original research. Library-based research is another term that is often used interchangeably with secondary research and, again, uses the data gathered by others. This term offers a timely reminder of the importance of spending time in the library (physically and virtually) as part of the research process. In this book the term desk-based research is used as distinct from secondary research and library-based research.

 DESK-BASED RESEARCH – finding your own data via indirect sources, often via the internet, without having direct contact with people.

SECONDARY RESEARCH – using data from previous studies to gain new insights and interpretations through a new research question.

LIBRARY-BASED RESEARCH – often an alternative term for secondary research.

Be careful to avoid the many websites that talk about desk-based research from a marketing perspective. Market research (what sells well and why) is not the same as doing a research project for a dissertation.

Why do desk-based research?

There are a variety of reasons why students undertake a desk-based study; sometimes it is because they want to, need to or are advised that this is the best way forward by their tutors. Here are examples of some of the reasons why students do desk-based research:

- Because of a particular interest in a sensitive area that would be difficult or unethical to research by gathering their own data. Examples include such things as experiences of suicide, abuse and bereavement.
- Because of a lack of confidence in gathering their own data. As new researchers, students can understandably be anxious about gathering their own data directly from people for a range of reasons, so choose to gather it from other sources instead.
- Because of unforeseen circumstances. This book was written during the COVID-19 pandemic, which prevented many students from carrying out things like their research interviews and focus groups. As a result, they had to do desk-based research instead.
- Because of the advice given by tutors. Tutors may advise students to carry out a desk-based study for a variety of reasons, some of which have already been mentioned. Sometimes it can also be to help a student on a practical level as desk-based research is generally much more predictable and, therefore, more manageable.

RAJESH

I'm really interested in the impact of music on mental health and wellbeing. I know it's always helped me at difficult times, and it would be great to find out what other people think about this. Originally, I planned to do a small number of semi-structured interviews with people on my course, but I guess I've become more and more anxious about doing this. I've suffered with anxiety issues in the past and I can tell my levels of anxiety are rising at the moment. I've talked to my supervisor about this and we've agreed I could explore this topic really well by doing desk-based research instead. This is a massive relief to be honest and now I can relax a bit and focus on what I need to do next.

Advantages and disadvantages of desk-based research

Like anything else, desk-based research has its advantages and disadvantages, and these will be explored now. Every research study needs to be managed well and, in general terms, the main advantage of this kind of research is that it is usually easier to manage because you can have a greater degree of control over it, which makes it more predictable (see Chapter 14). Many things can happen during an empirical study that are unexpected and situations (such as participants not responding to initial requests to take part, agreeing to take part but later no longer being able to or subsequently withdrawing their consent) are, unfortunately, all too common. This means an empirical study will have to be amended and maybe even done completely differently. On the whole, desk-based research carries much lower risk.

We have already alluded to the large amount of work involved in writing a dissertation. Many of my own students say that it is the biggest piece of academic work they have done so far, and their experiences tell me that it can easily 'mushroom'. Something that starts relatively small-scale can soon begin to feel that it is growing rapidly and getting out of control. A desk-based study is probably less likely to do this, although, of course, this is still perfectly possible.

Desk-based research opens up possibilities to study a particular area that simply would not be accessible otherwise. This might be because it could cause harm to participants, or to the researcher, or both (for example, by revisiting issues that have caused stress in the past). However, there are ethical dimensions to this kind of research that will be discussed in Chapter 10. Desk-based research also makes such things as a comparison of settings possible, including ones at home and abroad. For many students the idea of travelling abroad to gather data is impossible on a financial level and even travelling locally can be expensive. Desk-based research is invariably cheaper.

However, desk-based research also has its disadvantages. When researchers gather their own data, they do this in relation to the research question they have identified (see Chapter 5). But when gathering data from elsewhere, the material will often not have been intended for research purposes, which could mean that it is not as focused on a research question as it would be if you gathered the data yourself. This means taking great care with the data you select (see Chapter 7).

The quality of the data you collect is always important too. There are dangers in desk-based research of relying on poor-quality data and you need to avoid this wherever possible. Examples might be data that are too light which might not contain sufficient information (as in the case of short video clips) or data being set in a particular context which might be different from your own, such as a different geographical area or country. It will be important to have clear criteria to use when selecting your data as discussed in Chapter 7.

There may be some **copyright** issues when gathering data from the internet (see Chapter 10) and it will be important to consider these. It is also fair to say that there are times when things on the internet can literally disappear overnight and it will be vital to download and save data, and to know how you might be able to retrieve it should this happen (see Chapter 14). Table 1.1 summarises the advantages and disadvantages of desk-based research.

Table 1.1: Advantages and disadvantages of desk-based research

Advantages	Disadvantages
• Easier to manage because it is usually more predictable, so lower risk	• Can still be unpredictable, for example, data disappearing from the internet
• Easier to control the volume of data	• Data might not be as relevant as it could be to the project
• Opens up areas that it would not be possible to research otherwise	• There could be so many areas that it becomes vast and daunting
• Low risk of harm because data is gathered indirectly	• Data gathered may not be intended for research purposes
• Relatively inexpensive	• Data might be of poor quality

EMMA

I'd really like to do a piece of research to find out what makes people offend and reoffend. I can see it would be difficult to speak to offenders themselves and I've thought about interviewing prison officers instead, but I'm not sure that's what I want to do. I really want to hear the voices of the offenders themselves if I can, to try and understand more from their point of view. I'm going to consider doing some kind of desk-based project instead, but I'm not sure what this will involve at the moment.

The Research Triangle

Writers in the field of qualitative research methods often use the word iterative to describe key aspects of the process (for example, Maruster and Gijsenberg, 2012; Silverman, 2017; Hennink et al, 2020). An iterative process is a cycle that you repeat more than once, possibly even several times, and it can often feel like going back on yourself. This iterative cycle means being able to move regularly and flexibly between three key areas: your research question, the literature you are reviewing and your data. When I wrote *The Research Journal* (Bassot, 2020a) I used the concept of the Research Triangle to describe this, which is depicted in Figure 1.1.

I developed the Research Triangle while working with my students and this is how it works.

Figure 1.1: The Research Triangle

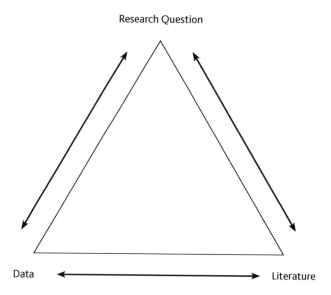

Research Question

Data   Literature

Research Question ↔ Literature (the right-hand side of the Research Triangle)

All research starts with a research question at the top of the Research Triangle (see Chapter 5) and this is usually included in a **research proposal**. It provides a focus for the study and gives initial ideas about what you are hoping to explore. This research question gives a sense of direction regarding what you need to start reading to build your literature review, hence the arrow from Research Question to Literature down the right-hand side of the Research Triangle. However, once you start your literature review you may not necessarily be able to find what you expected and in addition you might also discover some different, relevant and interesting things that surprise you. This means that you may well need to amend your research question in the light of what you have read; this is indicated by the arrow from Literature back to Research Question up the right-hand side of the Research Triangle.

Research Question ↔ Data (the left-hand side of the Research Triangle)

Your research question will also guide you to the data you need to collect; this is represented by the arrow from Research Question to Data down the left-hand side of the Research Triangle. As you gather the data, you won't always find what you expect to find, so again you may need to amend your research question; this is indicated by the arrow from Data back to Research Question up the left-hand side of the Research Triangle.

Data ↔ Literature (the base of the Research Triangle)

As you read more literature, you might find that other possible areas of focus related to your topic emerge, so you might decide to use some alternative data to support these, as shown by the arrow from Literature to Data along the base of the Research Triangle. Equally, your data might point you to some specific areas you now need to include in your literature review, as shown by the arrow from Data back to Literature along the base of the Research Triangle.

This iterative process can be tricky and even frustrating! Many people (including me) like to be able to complete a large task in a step-by-step way from start to finish, because it means they know where they are and can keep track of things. However, qualitative research often doesn't work like this, as the Research Triangle shows. It means being prepared to revisit things often to amend them as you go along in the light of what you are discovering. This also means that you can't write a dissertation from start to finish but will need to go back several times to redraft and refine your work, which can be challenging. Often it involves reworking sections that you felt were complete at the time as your work develops. Frustrating as this might be at times, it will probably lead to a better piece of work in the end. This iterative process is something you can reflect on either in your methodology section, or in a reflective **evaluation** of your research if you are asked to write one. Qualitative research is an iterative process. This means that your research question is a question in progress and not set in stone. You can, and probably will need to amend it, but you probably won't be able to change it completely. It might have gone through ethical clearance (see Chapter 4) and, in any case, there won't be time to do this.

 A research question is a work in progress and can be amended, but usually it can't be changed completely.

The Metaphorical Tent

The metaphor of a tent is used throughout this book to symbolise a research project leading to a dissertation. This is a traditional kind of tent that often takes some time to erect and which needs to be done in a methodical, step-by-step way to make it stable and secure. There are many similarities between the various parts of the Metaphorical Tent and the different aspects of doing a research project leading to a dissertation. The idea of a 'pop-up' tent-style dissertation is no doubt very attractive, but sadly in my view unrealistic! It is important to emphasise at this point that the Metaphorical Tent is what it says it is – a metaphor. So, it will not be totally accurate and if you are a knowledgeable and dedicated camper, please go with it. Many people enjoy camping and find it a fun and relatively inexpensive way of taking a holiday. However, not everyone likes camping, and I am one of them! Undoubtedly this is based on two negative past experiences of doing this in a traditional-style tent – the first in weather that was so hot that the ground felt like solid rock, and the second in heavy rain and storms where the tent leaked. While these are experiences I never want to repeat, they teach us some important lessons in relation to preparing the ground well and using good-quality camping equipment! The Metaphorical Tent is shown in Figure 1.2.

The Metaphorical Tent is made up of the following parts:

The tent poles – these need to be solid, located firmly on the ground and held in place by guy ropes to make them secure. They support the whole tent and if they are weak in any way, the entire tent may well collapse in difficult circumstances. These represent your research question.

The entrance to the tent – this is the only place where the tent needs to be flexible, so you can get in and out of it and, as such, represents the Research Triangle. It is also the introduction to your dissertation, the entrance to the whole piece of work.

The canvas on the right-hand side – this represents your literature review.

The canvas on the left-hand side – this is the data you collect and analyse.

The back of the tent – your conclusions.

The groundsheet – the whole tent stands on this and it represents desk-based methodologies.

The footprint groundsheet – this is an extra layer underneath the groundsheet that offers additional insulation while protecting the whole fabric of the tent. It represents a range of ethical considerations.

The guy ropes and tent pegs – these keep the whole tent rigid and secure, and a strong qualitative dissertation usually contains concise quotes from published authors (down the right-hand side) and from the data collected (down the left-hand side). In particular, the latter often bring a piece of work to life.

Throughout this book we will erect a strong, weatherproof Metaphorical Tent that will be robust enough to survive most things that nature (namely the research process and life more generally) might realistically throw at it. Unlike the tents I stayed in, it will not be built on ground that is so hard as to make the tent poles constantly fall over, or in such wet and windy weather that it leaks and feels like it could blow away at any moment!

Figure 1.2: The Metaphorical Tent

View from the front

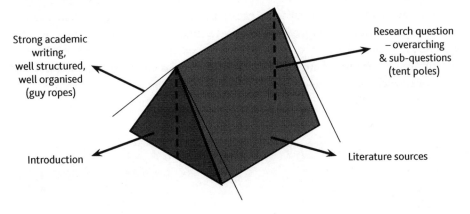

Strong academic
writing,
well structured,
well organised
(guy ropes)

Research question
– overarching
& sub-questions
(tent poles)

Introduction

Literature sources

View from the back

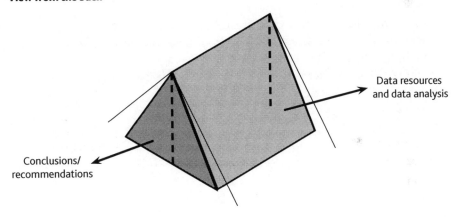

Data resources
and data analysis

Conclusions/
recommendations

View from beneath

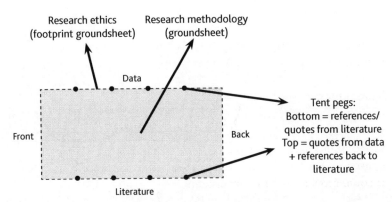

Research ethics
(footprint groundsheet)

Research methodology
(groundsheet)

Data

Front

Back

Literature

Tent pegs:
Bottom = references/
quotes from literature
Top = quotes from data
+ references back to
literature

SUMMARY

As you start thinking about your research project and your dissertation you might find that a desk-based study gives you lots of good options for your study. It might be that several of your friends are planning to do studies like this, or none of them, but either way it can be a good approach to take. We now continue preparing the ground for your Metaphorical Tent as we move on to Chapter 2 and the whole area of choosing a topic for your research project.

Further reading

Books devoted to desk-based research are relatively rare and here are two of the most useful ones I have come across:

- Largan and Morris (2019) offer an in-depth and very practical approach to doing a desk-based research project. It contains lots of diagrams and tables which make it visually helpful.
- Tight (2019) is another very helpful book on desk-based research. It is clearly laid out and also practical in its approach.

2

Choosing a topic

In this chapter we will:

☐ explore some definitions of **research**;

☐ discuss the importance of finding a topic that interests you and how to find it;

☐ start to look at some possible data resources;

☐ evaluate how to assess the size of your project;

☐ consider ways of making sure that your project is manageable in the time you have;

☐ examine the material that the Metaphorical Tent is made of.

This chapter focuses on the whole area of choosing a topic for your research project. This is an important first step in the research process and is a key element of getting ready to prepare the ground for erecting your Metaphorical Tent and involves considering the fabric that your tent is made of.

Choosing a topic is an interesting and exploratory phase, but in my experience, some students can find this difficult for various reasons. This means procrastination can set in and valuable time is lost (see Chapter 14). If you're in this position, this chapter should help you, but before we consider this in more detail, we need to start with another definition.

What is research?

No doubt your tutors will have already told you about the importance of including definitions in academic writing. Definitions often offer a very good starting point to a consideration of a topic as they show where the writer is coming from and can form part of a clear introduction to a piece of work. A dissertation is no different in this respect and you will probably want to consider including some definitions of relevant key terms in your introduction (see Chapter 6). Here we look at some definitions of research, including the distinction between the terms research and evaluation.

So, what is research? The *Oxford English Dictionary* (OED) defines the word research as both a noun and a verb:

- Noun – 'Systematic investigation or inquiry aimed at contributing to knowledge of a theory, topic, etc., by careful consideration, observation, or study of a subject.' Examples of the use of the word research as a noun include 'The students carried out research in ...' and 'Medical research shows that ...'
- Verb – 'To engage in research upon (a subject); to investigate or study closely.' Examples of the use of the word research as a verb include 'She researched the area of ... for her dissertation' and 'Researching this area was fascinating because ...'

In order to gain more understanding of what undertaking a research project involves, it is worth 'unpicking' the first definition by examining the OED's definitions of three key words contained within it.

- Systematic – here the OED uses words like 'deliberate intent', 'planned and organised method' and 'methodical'. This shows that research is thorough and well thought out, from the initial planning right through to the final write-up.
- Investigation – the OED defines this as an examination, which means that the subject is something that is looked at very closely and in detail.
- Inquiry – this is defined by the OED as something that is questioned and interrogated. It is in no way taking something for granted; in particular, the word interrogation implies very close scrutiny.

 Blaxter et al (2001: 5) use several of these words in their definition of research as 'diligent and systematic inquiry or investigation'.

Thomas (2017: 24) states clearly and succinctly what research is not. In his list he includes 'being committed to a position' and 'knowing something and trying to find "proof" for it'. I meet some students who seem to already know what they want to find even before their project begins. Inevitably this results in a predictable dissertation which leaves me thinking 'Well, they were always going to say that, weren't they?' Research is all about being open-minded regarding what you might find, even when (and perhaps especially when) it challenges your preconceived ideas.

Sometimes the terms research and evaluation are used together, which can be confusing. From the definitions considered so far we know that research involves a contribution to knowledge of a theory or topic. By contrast, evaluation is about determining the value or worth of something. For example, a piece of evaluation might seek to assess the value of a tutorial programme, by asking students what they enjoyed, didn't enjoy, found easy or difficult and so on. Following this, conclusions would be reached as to how effective the programme was. In this example, a piece of research would also involve a planned examination of the kind of support given, including a critical questioning of the approach being taken with reference to published literature. In the social sciences, especially the applied social sciences, evaluation will often form a part of a research study, but generally will not constitute the whole. In the example of the tutorial programme, the research study may well conclude with an evaluation of how effective the programme was, followed by some recommendations for practice.

RAJESH

I've known for quite a while now that music helps me when I'm under a lot of stress and I can see that it helps other people I know too. I'm starting to think about my topic and I want to know more about how effective music can be in alleviating stress. I've discussed it with my supervisor and they pointed out that at the moment my study sounds more like a piece of evaluation than a piece of research. They want me to delve deeper into which particular aspects of the topic I'm interested in finding out more about. They've also asked me to think about the theory that might inform my study. This is quite tough – I thought I knew what I was going to do, but I can see I need to do a bit of a rethink. Time to do more reading now, but I need to focus much more on the theory related to my topic.

The importance of identifying a topic

One of the first steps in the research process is to identify a topic. First and foremost, research requires **curiosity**; the well-known phrase 'curiosity killed the cat' does not really apply to research, but 'curiosity feeds the researcher' does. If you are curious to know more about an area, it could be something to research. The basis for this curiosity often comes from a deep and sustained interest in a particular area, so if you are interested in a topic, you will probably want to know more about it.

Always choose a topic you are interested in. This is the best way of being sure that your level of motivation is high, and it will keep you going for the duration of your project.

However, this interest alone may well not be enough. As well as being of personal interest, your topic area needs to be of interest to the academic community and will usually need to be one that has been researched before. A strong literature review will be an important part of your dissertation (see Chapter 8) and it will not be possible to write this unless your chosen topic area has been the subject of previous research and scholarship. In other words, you will need to be able to find a number of primary sources (see Chapter 1), for example, published books and academic journal articles that have been written on this area. Secondary sources such as textbooks, newspaper articles and websites might be useful, but an over-reliance on these will not give you the high mark you probably want.

The size of your topic must make your project manageable – big enough to 'get your teeth into' but not so big that it becomes overwhelming. You must be able to access data resources on the topic relatively easily (see Chapter 7) and the whole project must be practical and achievable in the time you have available. We discuss how to assess the size of your project in more detail later in this chapter.

Finding a suitable topic

So, how do you find a suitable topic? You can do this in a number of ways and some of these are better than others (see Figure 2.1). Here are some pointers:

- Something you have a personal interest in or are passionate about – if this links with your degree course, this can be a good place to start. You may have already found that you have a particular interest in something by following a blog or keeping your eye on particular websites. As you surf the internet you might be drawn to certain news items that raise particular issues. Any of these could guide you to a topic.
- One of your previous modules – for some students this is a really good starting point. Many (or even most) students find they enjoy some of their modules more than others and a topic that has a close link with a module they have particularly enjoyed can be a very good starting point to finding a focus for a research project. So, you could try going back to your favourite module and looking at the topics within it. It might be that as you do this something stands out to you as a possible area that you are still curious about, where you want to know more and that you are keen to delve more deeply into. Remember too that you will have done an amount of academic reading on this already, which could be very helpful when it comes to doing your literature review (see Chapter 8).
- The module where you got your highest mark – many students find they gain their highest mark in the module they enjoyed the most. If that's the case, again this could offer you a good indication of a possible topic. But if not, it might be good to avoid this area. A strong interest in a topic will sustain you through to completing a dissertation well; being academically strong in an area but without a definite interest in it may not.
- Wanting a particular supervisor – some students choose their topic because they want to work with a particular supervisor. This is a risky strategy on a number of levels. First, the supervisor's area of expertise might not be one that you are interested in or good at, so you could end up choosing something just for the supervisor. In addition, this supervisor might be so popular that there will be too many students for them to supervise. You might be one of the lucky students that gets this person as their supervisor, or you might not.
- The idea you had even before you started your degree – occasionally I meet a student who in year one knows what they want to do as their research project

Figure 2.1: Sources for a topic

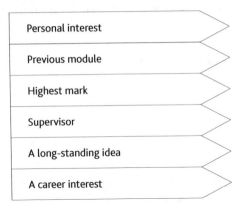

Personal interest

Previous module

Highest mark

Supervisor

A long-standing idea

A career interest

for their dissertation. In fact, it's probably the main reason they chose their degree course in the first place. If this is you, you obviously have a very strong interest in this area, so it is well worth pursuing.

- A career interest – sometimes students choose a topic because it relates to a career idea they are considering for the future. This gives them the opportunity to research it further and to become more knowledgeable about it. Further down the line, it all helps with the process of completing personal statements for applications for jobs and postgraduate study, as well as giving them lots to talk about at interview.

 If you choose a topic from your favourite module it could save you work, but you will need to be careful not to plagiarise yourself.

SAM

I guess I've always been interested in the experiences of refugees. Growing up, Mum told me so many stories of how she had to escape the war and flee for safety. It sounds like her life was so hard, and I admire her so much for what she did. It seems like an obvious topic to choose for my dissertation but there are so many aspects I'm interested in; it could be huge. And can I be objective about it? Or am I too emotionally involved? I'd love to speak to people directly about their experiences but I'm not sure I can do that because from what Mum has told me it might bring back too many bad memories for them. So, desk-based research seems like a good option for me. I've watched documentaries and read a lot about it already online but where do I start in trying to narrow things down?

Choosing a topic is always an important decision, so be careful not to rush into it. You can waste a lot of precious time by starting on a topic, changing your mind and needing to start again on a different one.

Where will I get my data from?

We will examine this question in detail in Chapter 7, but at this point it is important to begin to give this some careful thought. It goes without saying that if you choose a topic only to find later that you cannot access the data you need, you may find yourself needing to go back to 'square one'. This means you will have wasted a lot of time and you might then start to feel behind. At this point it is worth doing some general internet searching to see where your data might come from. You might be surprised to find that there are many data resources that can be used in a desk–based project; these have been put into the following three groups in Chapter 7 (see Figure 2.2):

1. written
2. visual
3. audio

It is well worth looking now to see the kinds of resources that are available that relate to your area of interest, so that you can be confident that you will be able to find what you need.

Figure 2.2: Types of data resources

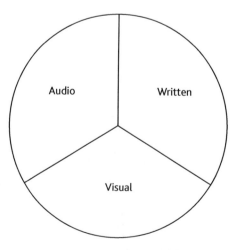

The size, scope and focus of your project

Both the size and scope of your topic are key issues to address to make sure that your research project is doable in the time you have available. Every research project also needs a clear focus; this will help you to keep 'on track' and not to deviate or digress into other areas. All researchers have to make decisions along the way about what they will cover and what they won't because otherwise most projects would be too big.

The size of a project is something that is often difficult to measure, especially in the early days. In addition, if you have a strong interest and some big ideas that come from it, you may find that your project quickly starts to expand. I often find myself saying to my own students things like 'But that's just too big' and 'How will you manage to do all of that before the deadline?' So, how do you assess the size of a project?

A good starting point is to do a brief outline plan. You may well be asked to do this as part of your research proposal (see Chapter 4), so doing it early on can help save you some time a bit later. At this stage it does not need to include lots of detail; a general overview can give you a good feel for whether or not you will be able to do what you want to do. Here is an example.

EMMA

I'm in my final year and it's the first semester. I'm doing my research methods module and will be doing my dissertation in semester two. This means I've got from the end of January until the beginning of May to do my dissertation. I've been thinking more about my topic and I definitely want to try and find out about why people offend and reoffend. At the moment I'm still not sure how I'll go about this but I'm thinking of using data from the websites of charities that work with offenders and ex-offenders to explore this whole area. I'm now trying to put together an outline plan for my research proposal. It's helping me assess the size of my project, and here is my first attempt.

Month	Tasks
January	Read websites from three major charities that work with offenders and ex-offenders
February	Find data and read relevant literature
March	Work on methodology
April	Analyse data
May	Do final write-up

I've realised there's a lot to do and if I organise it like this, I'll probably run out of time. I definitely need to do another plan!

Many students find that their topic is too big. Others find it is too narrow, not previously researched or simply not appropriate. If this turns out to be the case, do talk to your supervisor. Remember they want you to succeed and if they ask you to refine your choice of topic, they have your interests at heart and are not being a 'killjoy'!

 Talk to your supervisor if you are unsure about the size and focus of your topic.

How to narrow down the focus of a desk-based project

If your supervisor says your project is too big, how might you be able to narrow the focus down? Here are some common ways that this can be done that could help Sam and Emma:

- By geographical location – rather than looking nationally or internationally, you could narrow things down by examining a region or locality. This means that Sam could focus on refugees from a particular country, or those from a range of countries in a particular locality. Equally, Emma could focus on offenders in a particular region or area.
- By age range – you could focus on a particular age group (for example, young people aged 18–25, people over 50 or older people aged 65+) within your area of interest. Sam and Emma could concentrate on any of these age groupings for their projects.
- By ethnicity – you could get a much sharper focus by concentrating on people from a particular ethnic background. As stated previously, Sam may choose to focus the project on refugees from a particular country and Emma could concentrate on people from a particular ethnic group in her examination of offending.
- By gender – one way of literally halving your project is to carry out a gender-based study. Sam might choose to examine the experiences of male or female refugees while Emma might focus on male offenders. If she wants to narrow this down even further, she might choose females instead as they offend in much smaller numbers than men.
- By institution – this can be a very clear and helpful way of making sure that a project has definite boundaries. In desk-based research a relevant institution could be a college or university. Sam's project could include an examination of relevant policy documents published by educational establishments. Emma might focus on published data from particular prisons.
- By reducing the number of resources – students who undertake qualitative empirical studies often reduce the size of their projects by interviewing fewer participants. In a desk-based study it might be about focusing on fewer resources. For example, Sam and Emma might select their resources from the

websites of particular charities that seek to support refugees and offenders respectively. They could both choose fewer charities, which would reduce their workload very effectively.

If you do need to narrow down the focus of your study, whichever way you choose to do so is obviously up to you. Overall, your own particular interests are once again a good guide to help you to do this.

The Metaphorical Tent

Tents come in all sorts of different shapes and sizes and we know that the Metaphorical Tent is a traditional one. Tents are also made of different materials for different circumstances and weather conditions and these affect the tent's overall effectiveness and functionality. Writing a strong dissertation involves choosing a topic that will hold your interest for a significant length of time, so the Metaphorical Tent's material needs to be strong and durable. It also needs to be practical and doable, so not too heavy. It definitely needs to be waterproof to cope with the unexpected.

SUMMARY

Choosing a topic for your desk-based research is a key step in the process of beginning your study. Once you have begun to move forward with this you will also want to consider keeping a research journal, which can help you navigate the whole of the research process. This is another key aspect of preparing the ground for your Metaphorical Tent and we move on to this area in the next chapter.

Further reading

- Layder (2013) contains a very good chapter that considers seven interesting areas for research starting with popular culture (Chapter 2). The chapter includes a discussion of the different ways in which these could be researched and highlights some of the positives and possible challenges involved.
- Liu (2018) provides a clear discussion of the steps involved in choosing a research topic, from getting initial ideas to moving them forward into a possible research project.

3

Keeping a research journal

In this chapter we will:

☐ continue preparing the ground for your Metaphorical Tent;

☐ emphasise the importance of **criticality** at every point in the research process;

☐ discuss the role and purpose of a research journal in embedding **critical reflection** throughout your research project;

☐ explain the key terms **positionality** and **reflexivity** in qualitative research and how they help you address issues of subjectivity and **bias**;

☐ examine the characteristics of reflective writing;

☐ discuss a model for reflective writing to help you keep a research journal that will support you through the whole research process.

In this chapter we continue the process of preparing the ground for your Metaphorical Tent. Throughout, we consider the importance of critical reflection in every aspect of carrying out a robust desk-based research project and writing a dissertation that you can be proud of. This chapter will help you to write a research journal which will be an invaluable tool in enabling you reflect on each aspect of your project as it happens. A research journal also helps you to keep a record of things you will need to remember when you get to the 'writing-up' stage, building your knowledge and understanding as you progress. Again, we will start with some definitions.

What is criticality and why is it important?

By now, criticality is a term that you will probably have become familiar with during your time at university. It is often linked with skills such as analysis and evaluation. Criticality can also be seen as a state of mind or an approach to academic work in the following ways:

• we question everything, by asking things like 'Why?' and 'How do we know this?';

- we accept nothing 'at face value';
- we take nothing for granted;
- we don't accept anything as a 'given' despite how obvious it may seem.

Figure 3.1 illustrates a questioning approach. We can learn a lot about criticality from small children. They have a real thirst for new knowledge and understanding and are curious about everything they come across. This makes them experts in criticality. They ask the question 'Why?' not because they are criticising something, but simply because they want to understand more about it. At times they ask the question 'Why?' constantly, until their exhausted parent or carer finally says something like 'Because I say so!' In Chapter 2 we considered the great value in being curious about your topic and how this will 'feed' you during your project, keeping your motivation high.

Figure 3.1: A questioning approach

 Criticality is not the same as negative criticism. It means you are curious to know and understand more. It is a very positive skill to develop.

As well as having a deep level of curiosity, a critical mind is also very aware of the phrase 'Well, it depends …' This often points to issues of context and how something that on the surface can appear similar, yet can be experienced differently depending on the person and the situation. For example, why did some of your fellow students find one particular module difficult when perhaps you found it relatively easy? Having a critical mind means we are aware of our own strengths and weaknesses, we understand how we think and we can critique what we are learning as we are learning it.

Critical thinking lies at the heart of criticality and as your studies have progressed during your time at university, you will have gained the confidence to question everything, even those things you have previously accepted at 'face value' (Eales-Reynolds et al, 2013). In many academic areas, there is rarely a single correct answer; even in scientific disciplines, single solutions to complex problems can be difficult, and even impossible, to find. This was underlined throughout the COVID-19 pandemic, as we looked for answers when government advice based on emerging scientific evidence was constantly changing and sometimes was even conflicting.

Practising criticality is a key skill in doing well in your desk-based research project, and Thompson's (2012: 119) metaphor of 'helicopter vision' is very helpful in relation to this. Helicopters can fly in different ways depending on the circumstances. They can fly at a high level to give an overview of the landscape or terrain below. It means they can rise above a situation, hover over it and see the big picture. Equally, they can also fly low and descend to a very specific place to see things in detail and more clearly. Criticality in research involves both of these, seeing the big picture and the detail. For example, seeing the big picture will help when you write aspects of your introduction (see Chapter 6) and the detail will be relevant when carrying out a data analysis (see Chapter 11). Criticality can also help you to think creatively, which is particularly important for gaining the highest marks against university assessment criteria.

TIP Criticality is something we can all improve on. Don't be afraid to do some kind of refresher course provided by your university library or study support centre. It could make all the difference when it comes to writing a dissertation you can be proud of.

What is a research journal?

A research journal is a reflective tool that can help you develop your knowledge and understanding throughout your desk-based research project. During your time at university you might have been asked to keep some kind of reflective journal. This is particularly the case if you are on an applied professional course such as teaching, social work or nursing, or if you have done a work placement. You might also have been asked to write some reflective pieces of assessed work and both of these experiences will help you when writing a research journal.

Even so, many students ask me how they can be sure that they are writing reflectively. In order to recognise this, you need to understand the general characteristics of reflective writing, which are as follows (and here they are applied to the research process).

Reflective writing is different from other kinds of academic writing and is:

- always written in the first person (I ...), with a focus on you and your learning and development through the vehicle of your research project;
- often more personal than other forms of academic writing;
- private and not seen by anyone else;
- evaluative, not descriptive, so not just what you did during your project but how and why, and giving consideration to the strengths and weaknesses in your approach;

- about getting beneath the surface of what happened by examining your experiences, thoughts, feelings and **assumptions** about your project;
- a form of self-supervision and a means of 'offloading', which can help reduce your stress levels;
- honest and spontaneous;
- subjective, so there are no right or wrong answers;
- a record of your thoughts and experiences that you can return to throughout your project, especially when you get to the writing-up stage;
- an investment of time in your own academic learning and development.

So, reflective writing is not simply about describing what happened. It is analytical and helps us to link our ideas together and discover meanings from the things we see and experience. This means we build new knowledge as our understandings become broader and deeper as we question everything, and it is a tool for developing our critical thinking.

 Writing in a research journal takes time, but is time well invested.

SAM

My supervisor keeps saying I should keep a research journal, but I've never done this before. I still don't really understand why I need to do this, but my supervisor seems to be good so I guess I need to at least give it a go. I think an easy place for me to start is thinking more about my mum's experiences. I can't really imagine what her life must have been like before she came to this country, but I know she must have been so grateful to feel safe and secure here – something that I completely take for granted every single day. It was so hard for her, but she got a new life and so did I.

Why keep a research journal?

Many people in universities understand the value of journal writing and recognise that it can help students in various areas of their academic and personal development. Most tutors on research methods courses recommend that students keep a research journal and here are some of the reasons why (see Figure 3.2):

- It helps us to slow down – developing critical thinking takes time and writing in a journal gives us a focus for this.
- It helps to externalise things – spending too long thinking about things means that they can start going round and round in our heads (including in bed!).

Figure 3.2: Reasons for keeping a research journal

Over time, this can make us feel confused and overwhelmed. Writing in a journal gets our thoughts out on paper, and often our heads then feel clearer as a result, which then helps us to make progress and even get back to sleep.

- It's a place for 'offloading' – all research has its ups and downs, and a journal can be a great place for articulating our feelings, particularly when things don't go according to plan. This helps us to cope with the stressful parts of a project and to deal with our levels of anxiety more generally.
- It helps us to 'keep on track' – most of us need to plan in order to succeed, hence the well-known phrase 'to fail to plan is to plan to fail' (see Chapter 14). A journal can be a secure place (definitely more secure than a piece of paper that we can lose) for our research plans.
- It provides us with a record that we can refer back to – most of us can fool ourselves into thinking that we will remember things, particularly when it is something significant. Unfortunately, everyday life and study are hectic, a research project can be large and we simply can't remember everything. Sometimes even important things can escape our memory.
- It helps us to question our assumptions – taking a questioning approach to journal writing involves critical thinking and can help us to address issues of subjectivity and bias in our research (see Chapter 10).
- It makes us accountable to ourselves – a good supervisor (see Chapter 13) will want to know about the progress we are making, but the progress we make will always be down to us. Keeping a journal means that we can keep a check on ourselves, for example, where we are in the process and what we need to do next.

Journal writing can be done in a number of ways (for example, by hand in a notebook or on a device such as a smartphone or tablet). However, the value of writing by hand should not be underestimated. Research in neuroscience shows that it stimulates a particular part at the base of the brain called the reticular activating system, or the RAS (Pérez Alonso, 2015). The RAS acts as a filter for information that the brain needs to process and ensures that we pay more attention to what we are actively focusing on at a given moment. So, writing sharpens our focus and is usually a more effective way of learning than typing, discussion or reading. This means that you will be much more likely to remember something you have written down than something you have typed, read or discussed.

Writing by hand always involves making decisions about what to write, which means processing your thoughts and expressing yourself in words; this helps your understanding to develop. For example, when doing your literature review (see Chapter 8) if you decide to take notes from one of your readings, simply copying the text might not help you to understand it, but summarising it and putting it into your own words probably will. So, the act of writing helps us to develop our understanding. As one professor I knew well put it, 'I write in order to understand, not because I understand something already.' This is illustrated extremely well by Adams St. Pierre (2005) in her section 'Writing as a method of nomadic enquiry' where she discusses the role of writing in qualitative research. She states, 'a great part of that inquiry is accomplished in the writing because, for me, writing *is* thinking, writing *is* analysis, writing *is* indeed a seductive and tangled *method* of discovery' (Adams St. Pierre in Richardson and Adams St. Pierre, 2005: 1423).

However, today most of us use some kind of keyboard more than we write by hand and many of us can type quicker than we can write. So, do we really need to write by hand? Evidence from an interesting study by Mueller and Oppenheimer (2014) showed that students who used laptops for taking their lecture notes produced poorer-quality work than those who took notes by hand. Those using laptops often tried to type every word the lecturer said, but students who wrote by hand had to be much more selective about what they wrote. This meant they had to start processing the material straight away and this is what helped them to perform better in their studies. So, writing by hand does seem to have some benefits. But if you have a particular learning support need (for example, dyslexia) using a keyboard might be a much better option. Don't be afraid to experiment and always make sure you do what suits you best.

RAJESH

This is great! I've kept a journal now for a long time because it helps me deal with my anxieties. And now I need to keep one for my course, so this is going to be easy for me. I guess it's reminded me too that music has always helped with my anxieties. Seems like this could well be why I want to do this project – that's part of the positionality thing for me. But there's no getting away from it – doing my dissertation feels like a really big thing and I can already feel it beginning to grow even bigger in my mind.

Doing this journal will be a great way of offloading – getting my thoughts out of my head and down on paper – what a relief! I know it will help and it will also be a great way to keep me on track.

What does a research journal look like?

On the surface this sounds like a simple enough question but delve a little deeper and it's not necessarily as easy as it sounds. This is because people do not always agree on what a research journal should look like, and in fact there are views that seem to be at extreme opposites. Some see it as a place to take brief notes, primarily in relation to sources (for example, books, journal articles) and others seem to say you should keep a record of everything! Most people advocate writing in it regularly but are much less clear about what you should write. My own publication (Bassot, 2020a) gives lots of helpful advice and tips on keeping a research journal, as well as guiding you through each step of the research process. I often advocate writing little and often; you might be surprised how much you can achieve by writing for 15 minutes twice a week. This kind of writing can be done anywhere: on the bus or train, in a coffee shop and so on.

In relation to journal writing, the words journal, diary and log are sometimes used interchangeably, which can be confusing. These three terms tend to mean different things as follows:

- Journal – this is often a place for free-flowing writing. Some people are avid journal writers and keep a personal journal every day where they write about their lives. Others decide to keep a journal for a specific purpose, for example, for a project or during their travels. In everyday life a journal often takes the form of a nice quality notebook where you can write freely. It can also be used as a place to keep other things, such as photographs, diagrams and lists. Initially most of the pages will probably be blank.
- Diary – this tends to be calendar-driven with specific dates listed and there are a variety of options to choose from (for example, a week to view on each page, a week spread across two pages); it will often include planners for the month or year. There will also be space to write, but this is often relatively small and means you feel you have to restrict your writing to the amount of space given, which is not always helpful.
- Log – this is a basic record of events, often kept in date order. It is generally factual, so a list of what you did and when.

Famous writers of journals, diaries and logs:
Journal – Leonardo da Vinci, Marie Curie, Frida Kahlo
Diary – Samuel Pepys, Charles Darwin, Anne Frank
Log – Captain Scott (of the Antarctic), Captain Kirk (Star Trek)

As you undertake your research project, you are likely to need all three of these forms in order to make your research journal work for you. Free-flow writing will help your ideas and understanding to develop. This could be prompted by things like reading texts that you feel are key to your research, discussions with your supervisor, things you discover as you gather your data and so on. Diary aspects will be particularly helpful for planning (see Chapter 14), as this will keep you on track and you will be less likely to lose sight of what you need to do and by when. A log will ensure that you can find things quickly and easily, such as those all-important references. How you choose to keep a research journal is up to you, so feel free to use it in the way it helps you most.

More key terms

Keeping a research journal helps us in a variety of ways during the qualitative research process, particularly in relation to two key areas.

1. Reflexivity – this is a potentially confusing term as it might suggest some kind of reflex action; in fact, it's the opposite. Reflexivity in research is defined as the ability to see the things that are influencing our thoughts, behaviours and actions (Fook and Askeland, 2006), so it's about recognising our preconceived ideas about things. This involves a high level of self-awareness and is achieved through a deep level of critical reflection. Reflexivity in research means we are open-minded, and it protects us from making lots of assumptions. This is different from reflection which is a term used to describe the thinking processes we engage in as learners, and reflectivity that is the deliberate action of thinking analytically (Bassot, 2020b).
2. Positionality – reflexive researchers are clear about where they stand on key aspects of their study. In Chapter 1 we saw that in qualitative research there is no single correct answer or solution, only insights and interpretations. Finley (2008) argues that the knowledge we have is situated in a cultural setting and is always influenced by our social context. All researchers come to a project with ideas and thoughts they already have on a topic and these will have been influenced by a range of social factors, including prior knowledge and experience. Bearing in mind that most people choose a topic that they already have an interest in, this is not surprising. Positionality means being clear about where we stand in relation to our research, including any assumptions we might be making. Many qualitative dissertations include a positionality statement, which can be included either as part of an introduction or a methodology section. We will discuss this further in Chapters 6 and 9.

Keeping a research journal can go a long way in ensuring that we remain reflexive and continue to understand our preconceived ideas and assumptions in relation to a research study. Most importantly, it helps us address issues of bias.

Keeping a research journal helps us to be aware of our assumptions and means we are much less likely to write a dissertation where the marker thinks 'Well, they were always going to say that, weren't they?'

The Integrated Reflective Research Cycle

Most people who are new to reflective writing find it helpful to use some kind of structure to help them get going. This model is designed to help you as you start to complete a research journal for your desk-based project. It is based on my Integrated Reflective Cycle (Bassot, 2020b), which applies the work of a number of writers on the whole area of reflective practice (Kolb, 1984; Gibbs, 1998; Johns, 2004). If you are studying on a professional course (such as nursing, teaching or social work) you may well have come across some of these before.

The Integrated Reflective Research Cycle (IRRC) is shown in Figure 3.3 and is a tool designed to help you examine what you are doing closely. At each point on the cycle there are a number of questions you can ask, which help you to develop your skills of criticality. You can use the cycle at various points during your research project, for example, at the beginning to help you start to write reflectively, during your project to monitor your progress and at the writing–up

Figure 3.3: The Integrated Reflective Research Cycle

What happened?
What did I do?
What were the contributory factors?

What will I do next time?

How could I do better next time?

What will I now consider for next time?

What strategies can I adopt to move forward?

The Experience

Preparation   *Reflection-in-action*   Reflection-on-action

Theory

What was I trying to achieve?

Why did I do what I did?

What assumptions did I make?

What were the consequences for my research?

How did I feel?

How has this contributed to my knowledge of my topic?
How has it confirmed what I already knew?
What do I know now that I didn't before?

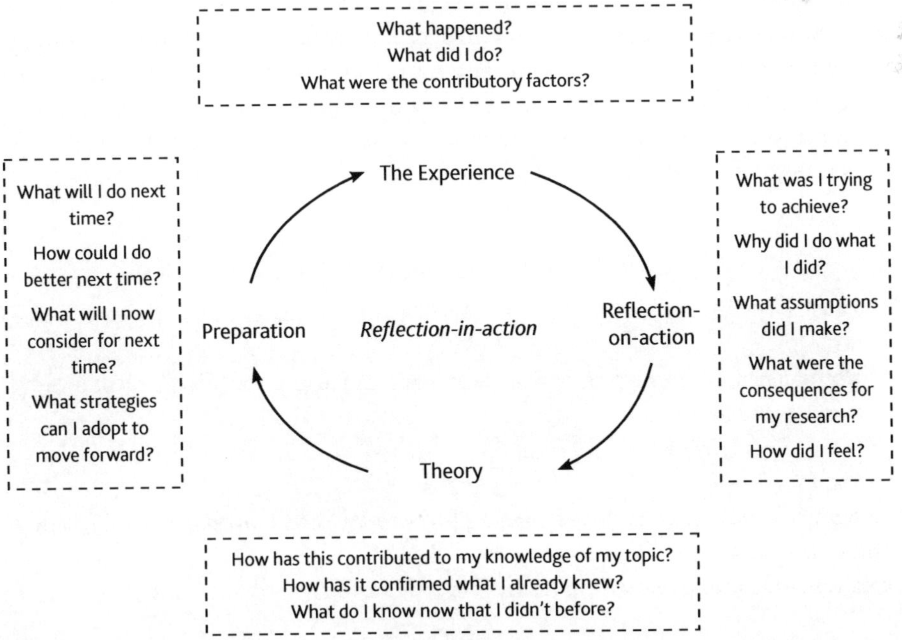

stage. Whenever you use it, working through all four stages on the cycle will help you to interrogate what you are doing by taking a questioning approach.

Starting at the top, the first point on the IRRC is The Experience and involves describing what you did, or what happened. This helps you keep a record and can be a relatively easy starting point for your reflective writing. It includes a prompt to think about the contributory factors – the things that might have influenced what happened, such as the time and place, the circumstances, your mood and even the weather. It is a reminder to think about a range of different things that might have had an impact on what you did.

The second point on the cycle is Reflection-on-action (Schön, 1983). This is all about thinking back on what you did and reviewing it. It includes a range of questions to help you explore your motivations, feelings and any assumptions you might have been making. This may well be the longest part of the IRRC and is well worth taking some time over.

The third point is Theory and relates to your developing knowledge in relation to your topic. Here the focus is on how your research confirms what you already knew (for example, when you started your project) and what you know now. Keeping a note of the differences will enhance your level of critical thinking.

The fourth point is Preparation, which helps you continue to move forward in the research process. It is well worth taking some time to address the questions raised here to keep your thinking and planning sharp and in focus. These questions will also be particularly helpful when evaluating your research as part of your conclusions and recommendations (Chapter 12).

In the centre of the IRRC is the term Reflection-in-action (Schön, 1983); this is the capacity that we all have as human beings to think about things while we are doing them. Schön likens this to the well-known phrase 'thinking on your feet' and it is something we all do all the time. In other words, thoughts about a research project can occur any time and it is well worth trying to take note of them whenever you can as they could inform your overall thinking. Using a small notebook or recording these on your smartphone can be very helpful.

EMMA

Not finding this journal writing thing very easy, so I'm going to have a go at using the IRRC today.

The Experience – went to the library to start looking for literature on why people reoffend. I got really confused – there's just so much and I just don't know where to start.

Reflection-on-action – I was trying to make a good start and thought the library would be a good place to go. I definitely assumed it would be easy and it's made me feel a bit confused and I think I've started to panic a bit.

Theory – my knowledge is really growing now and this is going to be more difficult than I thought. Looks like I'll need to narrow down my focus even further.

Preparation – just as I was leaving, I bumped into someone from my group. They said that people in the library are always helpful if you can't find what you need and even when you don't know what you're looking for! I remember my supervisor saying that it's a good idea to book a session with someone in the library for help. I'm definitely going to do this as soon as I can.

SUMMARY

In this chapter we have considered a range of issues in relation to the value of keeping a research journal. Writing is a key part of enabling our understanding to grow and a research journal is a great tool to aid us in this. Trying different approaches is a good way of finding what works for you, so be prepared to give things a go and you may well reap the benefits. In the next chapter we focus on the final aspect of preparing the ground as we examine the whole area of writing a strong research proposal.

Further reading

- Bassot (2020a) is my own guide to keeping a research journal and includes activities and tips to help you get the most from journaling.
- Bolton and Delderfield (2018) is a book you will enjoy if you enjoy reflective writing. Chapter 7 is good for people who are new to it and includes sections on writing to learn and finding your writer's voice.

4

Writing a strong research proposal

In this chapter we will:

☐ discuss the purpose of a research proposal;

☐ explore what a research proposal looks like;

☐ examine the component parts of a research proposal and liken these to different parts of the Metaphorical Tent;

☐ discuss the characteristics of strong and weak research proposals;

☐ consider some practical tools you might use when writing your proposal.

The purpose of a research proposal

In many academic disciplines, the first step towards doing a piece of research is to complete a research proposal. This is what it says it is, a proposal, so it shows what you are proposing to explore in your study. It is completed before the research starts and is usually a relatively brief discussion of what you plan to do to reach the final point of submitting your dissertation. Denscombe (2019) offers the following seven key questions to describe what a research proposal should contain:

1. What is the study about?
2. What do we know already?
3. What do we want to find out?
4. How will we do this?
5. How long will it take?
6. Will it be done in an ethical way?
7. What could the outcomes be?

(Adapted from Denscombe, 2019: 5)

If you are studying for an undergraduate degree and doing, or planning to do, a dissertation module, you are likely to be asked to write a research proposal. You could be asked to do this as part of a research methods module or as part of your dissertation module; it varies. You could be doing a research methods module during your final year or in your penultimate year; that varies too. In any case writing a research proposal is a good thing because it provides you with an opportunity to do some forward thinking and planning.

Research proposals have a number of very useful purposes and here my TESS model (see Figure 4.1) is useful:

- *Thoughts* – when you are starting to think about a large piece of academic work, it is helpful to get your early thoughts down on paper as it often means that you begin to see the way forward. Many students find these early stages in the process confusing and even overwhelming, and it can be easy to get lost and to be unclear about where to start. A proposal can be a really helpful way of beginning to see what lies ahead.
- **Ethics** *and safety* – this is an important part of the process that we cover in detail in Chapter 10. All research must be carried out ethically and the same applies to desk-based research. Research must be done with due regard to your own safety and that of the data you use. Your proposal might be checked by people in your department (often called the ethics committee or panel) and, if so, this is a way of safeguarding you, your data and the people who have shared it. It gives you confidence that what you are doing is sound and safe.
- *Suitability* – the proposal helps you to begin to assess whether or not your project is suitable for a dissertation. In selecting a topic, you will have chosen something that is of interest to the academic community (see Chapter 2) and writing your proposal will help you to revisit this. This will give you confidence in your topic as you move forward. Walliman (2014: 68) argues that 'A good proposal will indicate how your chosen topic emerges from issues that are being debated within your subject field, and how your work will produce a useful contribution to the debate.'
- *Size* – writing a proposal helps you begin to assess the size of your project. As part of the process you may need to write a plan of what you will do and when. This is all part of good project management, which we discuss in Chapter 14. At this point, the size of your project is still a subjective thing, but it is something that you will start to get a feel for as you write your proposal. Many of my own students say things like 'this feels as if it's going to be too big now' as they write their proposals and it helps them to become more focused.

Figure 4.1: The TESS model

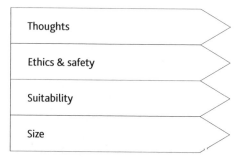

RAJESH

I'll need to write my research proposal soon, so I'm going to try using the TESS model in my research journal to try and make a start.

Thoughts – I suppose I've been interested in music for as long as I can remember. My mum said I was one of those kids that learned how to sing and talk at the same time. I even used to make up songs! I've always found music so relaxing too. I guess I've wanted to do this study for quite a long time when I look back.

Ethics and safety – talking to people directly about their anxieties might make them feel even more vulnerable. I know I wouldn't want to do it if someone asked me. It might affect me too because of my own experiences. So, I've decided to do a desk-based study instead. It makes me realise though that, although I really want to do this study, I might read some disturbing stuff. I'll need to look after myself and make sure I talk to people, so I don't bottle things up.

Suitability – looking in the library there's a lot of academic literature on the role of music and issues of anxiety. There are stories online of people who have found it helpful, so getting data should be quite easy. There's also a lot on music therapy and how it can be used with many different people.

Size – lots of literature and data resources make me feel like my project could be quite big – maybe too big. I need to get a handle on what I can and can't do. What's too big and how can I be sure not to get overwhelmed? Is my project about music therapy? I don't think so at the moment, but I think I need to at least consider it even if I decide it isn't. I think writing some kind of timeline will help me get more of an idea of what's doable in the time I have.

Now try using my TESS model in your own research journal.

What does a research proposal look like?

Many universities ask students to complete some kind of template when submitting their research proposal. Often this can make writing your proposal much easier than writing an assignment. Through your research methods or dissertation module, it should be clear if your university is asking you to use a particular template to write your proposal and, if not, do be sure to ask. The proposal template (or form) will probably be on your module or course

Virtual Learning Environment (VLE). There might also be a copy on your university's website.

 If you are in any doubt about whether or not you need to use a template, or about which template to use, be sure to ask.

Finding and using the correct template for your research proposal shouldn't be difficult, but it can be confusing. And, you can waste a lot of valuable time using the wrong one, which can be very frustrating! If in doubt, ask someone (preferably a member of academic staff) before you start so you can be sure.

 There might be different templates for different courses. There might also be templates for undergraduate, postgraduate masters and doctoral-level students. Be sure to read them carefully and use the right one.

Writing a proposal might be similar to some of the writing you have done already at university, especially if you have had to write reports or reflective assignments, but it will probably be different from most of your academic writing so far. If you are asked to use a template or form, this will be very different from writing an assignment and many students find this easier because it offers a very clear structure. Sometimes these templates specify how many words each section should contain, and overall a proposal will be a shorter piece of writing than an essay, typically, 2,000 to 2,500 words. Any research proposal is a work in progress and lays out your intentions for the future. It is not 'set in stone' and is part of the process of keeping an open mind. This means that it is always best written in the future tense because it is about what you are intending to do.

 Always write your proposal using the future tense, because it is literally what you are proposing to do at this stage.

Templates for research proposals differ but they also have a lot of common elements. Most contain the following sections, which are adapted here for a qualitative desk-based study:

- title
- brief description of proposed study
- research questions
- literature sources
- research design, methodology and data analysis

- data resources
- ethical issues to be considered
- project timescales

 At this point it is well worth finding your university's proposal form and comparing the content of it with these bullet points.

The elements of a research proposal

We will now examine each of the elements in the list that go towards making a research proposal, remembering that this is what you are proposing to do and that it is not 'set in stone'. We will link each of them where relevant with the component parts of the Metaphorical Tent (see Figure 4.2).

Title – this is part of your entrance to your Metaphorical Tent. It might seem very early to decide on a title for your project and, in fact, it is. What is needed at this point is an idea of what you think your title might ultimately be. Often the title will be one of the last things you decide, as it might only become clear much further down the line. In qualitative research, this often happens as part of the process of data analysis (see Chapter 11). A good title tempts the reader into the whole piece and makes them think something like 'this looks really interesting'. So, at this point, don't feel that you have to spend lots of time trying to think of a good title. Later on, it may become clear, even obvious, and we will revisit this in Chapter 12.

 It's well worth making a note of any possible titles as they occur to you. If not, you might forget them, which can be very frustrating!

Brief description of proposed study – this is another part of the entrance to your Metaphorical Tent and could form part of your introduction (see Chapter 6). It is a good opportunity to write a short number of words as a clear outline of your study. It will contain the words desk–based and qualitative and will probably include a concise description of your topic area and what you intend to do. It might raise a current and pertinent issue, showing some of the reasons for your interest in carrying out research in this area.

Research question(s) – these are your tent poles, and this is the place to write your overarching question, broken down into a small number of sub-questions (see Chapter 5).

Figure 4.2: The Metaphorical Tent and your research proposal

View from the front

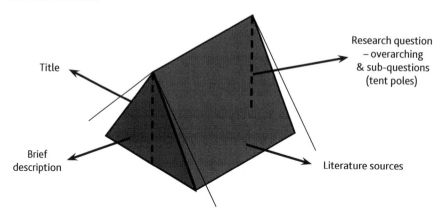

View from the back

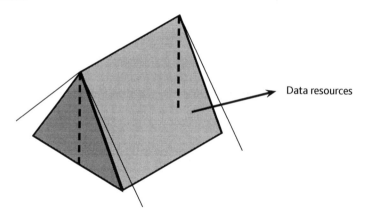

View from beneath

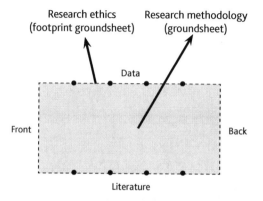

Literature sources – this is the canvas on the right-hand side (see Chapter 8). You have already identified that your topic is of interest to the academic community and by now you may well have selected a small number of readings that will be relevant for your study. If you are an avid reader, you may well have identified more than that! But at the moment you only need to give an indication of what you will read. Obviously, you won't have read everything yet and the expectation is that you give some examples. It is helpful to put them into groups and one good way of doing this is to try and identify three or four themes in the literature that seem important at the moment in relation to your research question, and to give a small number of examples underneath each of them. Don't forget that one of the themes needs to cover the whole area of research methods as covered in your research methods module. This literature will form an important part of your justification for your methodology.

Research design, methodology and data analysis – this is the groundsheet and we will cover this in detail in Chapter 9. This section is likely to include several important words including methodology, **epistemology**, interpretivism, **ontology** and **subjectivism**. Don't worry if you don't understand them now, as they are words you might not have come across before. Here you will also need to include how you might plan to analyse your data. This can be especially difficult to conceptualise at this point as it often becomes clearer as the project progresses, when you collect the data and become immersed in it (see Chapter 11). For now, it will probably be enough to suggest possible approaches (for example, **thematic analysis**).

Data resources – this is the canvas on the left-hand side. By now you will probably have started to look for some possible online data resources for your study. But you don't need to be specific here as you will not yet have found all of them or the most relevant ones; some examples will do. It will be useful though to highlight the type or types of resources you will draw on, for example, written, video and/or audio, and how you might select them.

Ethical issues to be considered – this is the footprint groundsheet and we will examine this in Chapter 10. These may well include issues of privacy and **confidentiality**. You will probably also need to consider your own safety and security. You could also include a discussion of why you decided to do a desk-based study and the ethical issues that you can avoid because of this.

Project timescales – this is one of the most useful parts of the proposal in that it demands a closer look at what you will do and by when. In Chapter 2, Emma has a first go at doing this. Including a bit more detail in your proposal might be useful.

SAM

My ideas are progressing well and it's now time to start writing my proposal. I need to use the university's template, but for now I'm going to write some notes using these headings. I know my proposal needs to be about 2,000 words long.

Project title: Issues experienced by refugees

Brief description of proposed study (including the area to be addressed and its significance)	This study will explore some of the experiences of refugees and the impact of these on their lives. The issues they face could include culture shock, confusion, feeling homesick, missing friends and relatives, language barriers and unemployment.
Research question(s)	What issues do refugees experience?
	Which factors seem to affect them?
	What support might refugees need?
Literature sources	Experiences of refugees – identify books and academic journal articles
	Support for refugees – identify websites of relevant charities, government departments and local councils
	Research methods – identify core books on desk-based research
Research design, methodology and data analysis	The research will be a desk-based study using the published biographies of refugees as a data resource. The study will interpret the stories of the refugees using the research questions, so its methodology will be interpretivist. The data analysis will use a narrative approach.
Data resources	Published biographies of refugees
Ethical issues to be considered	Desk-based in order not to cause harm to any refugees. Self-care in relation to hearing more about their experiences which could be similar to my mum's. Contact personal tutor for support if needed. Consider relevant copyright issues.
	Self-care – I might find the biographies upsetting and if so, will seek support from student wellbeing services.
Project timescales	Month 1 – read biographies and take notes, keep research journal and write notes on methodology
	Month 2 – literature review and data analysis
	Month 3 – write methodology
	Month 4 – finish writing literature review and data analysis, plus introduction and conclusion

What makes a strong proposal?

Earlier we discussed that a research proposal may be similar to things you have already written while at university (such as reports) but will also probably be different. Here are some characteristics of a strong proposal:

- Written in the future tense – remember that this is what you will (probably) be doing, so the future tense is the most appropriate. It includes words like will, shall and may.
- Written in the first person – this is your study, so do write about it in the first person (I will …)
- Written on the appropriate template or form – if you are asked to write your proposal in a particular format, do please comply with this. There are no 'brownie points' to be gained for 'doing your own thing' and, in fact, you could lose valuable marks if you don't because you might not meet the relevant assessment criteria.
- Concise – a proposal might be one of the shortest assignments you will write at university. If you are using a template or form, follow the guidance for the whole and for each section in relation to the word count. They are there to guide you.

In their excellent guide on writing an undergraduate research proposal, the University of Bradford suggests using the WHITTLE checklist as a way of assessing the quality of your proposal.

What: is the research question – is it targeted and refined or too broad?

How: will you carry out your research – what is the methodology, methods and tools you have chosen and why? Why have you rejected others? What is your stance as a researcher?

Importance: why is your research important? Who are the people most likely to find your research important?

Timely: why should your research be carried out now?

Title: does your proposed title tell a reader what the research is about?

Literature: have you identified the key research carried out in your field? Do you show a clear link between the existing literature and your research?

End result: are the aims clearly defined and when you have finished your research, what will the end result be? (University of Bradford, nd: 8)

Tools for writing a research proposal

Some students find it helpful to use some kind of tool when writing their research proposal. These may well include things you have used in the past and here are three examples.

Flow charts

A **flow chart** is a diagram that shows the steps you will take to write your dissertation. It helps you to see the whole project broken down into its constituent parts. It can be particularly helpful if you need to get an impression of the research process. It can also show the links between different aspects of your project. Here is an example in relation to Sam's research (see Figure 4.3).

Figure 4.3: Sam's flow chart

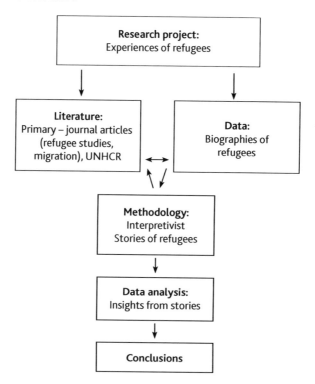

Mind maps

Mind maps were invented by Tony Buzan in the 1970s as a result of hosting a TV series called *Use Your Head*. A mind map (Buzan and Buzan, 2010) is a diagrammatic representation of a complex thing (such as a research project) that shows the links between its various aspects. Mind maps have become very popular in many areas of life, personal, business and academic. Many people use them and find them very effective in literally mapping out a project. If you respond well to visual things, you may well find a mind map for your research project helpful. It's something that you could print off and have above your desk as well as on your smartphone or tablet and could act as a very useful reminder of your whole project and the more specific aspects of it.

EMMA

I'm thinking about my research proposal now and might try using a mind map. I use them quite a lot on my course and find they help me to visualise things. So I'm going to have a go and see how I get on.

Figure 4.4 shows Emma's first attempt at a mind map for her study.

Figure 4.4: Emma's mind map

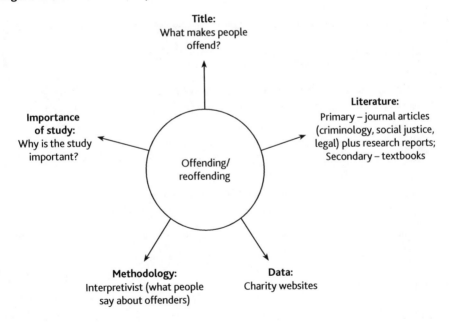

Gantt charts

A **Gantt chart** is a visual representation of tasks you need to undertake and actions you need to complete in order to write your dissertation. These are displayed against time; see Figure 4.5, which relates to Rajesh's research. On the left–hand side of the chart is a list of activities he needs to complete and along the top is an approximate timescale.

Figure 4.5: Rajesh's Gantt chart

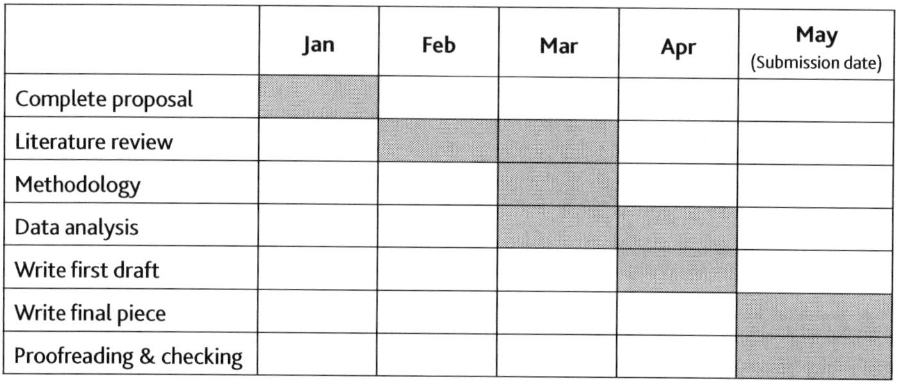

	Jan	Feb	Mar	Apr	May (Submission date)
Complete proposal	▓				
Literature review		▓	▓		
Methodology			▓		
Data analysis			▓	▓	
Write first draft				▓	
Write final piece					▓
Proofreading & checking					▓

SUMMARY

In this chapter we have considered the whole process of completing your research proposal. This helps you to ensure that you understand everything you need to erect your Metaphorical Tent. Writing a proposal is an important part of the research process and it will be a very useful working document to have throughout the whole period of writing your dissertation. We have now reached the end of Part I of the book and in the next chapter we move on to look at issues of context and background, along with how to write a good introduction to a desk-based study.

Further reading

- Denscombe (2019) provides a clear and accessible book dedicated to the whole area of writing a research proposal based around his seven questions.
- Walliman (2014) contains a very good chapter on how to write a strong research proposal and takes a practical, systematic approach.

PART II

Assembling the structure

In Part II we move on to erecting your Metaphorical Tent. This begins with making sure your tent poles (your research question and sub-questions) are secure and then we focus on each aspect of the canvas. These represent the context, background and introduction to your research, how to select high-quality data resources for desk-based research and your literature review. Other important aspects are desk-based methodologies and a consideration of the importance of taking an ethical approach to your study, which represent the groundsheets. We finish putting the canvas over the tent poles by considering some different techniques of data analysis and writing strong conclusions and recommendations. We continue to follow Sam, Emma and Rajesh's progress as they work on their projects and write their dissertations.

5

The importance of
your research question

In this chapter we will:

☐ discuss the importance of your research question using the image of the Metaphorical Tent;

☐ consider how you can move forward from identifying a topic to devising a research question;

☐ examine what makes a good research question;

☐ discuss how to devise a good research question;

☐ create some criteria to use when assessing your research question;

☐ explain the flexible nature of a research question in qualitative research.

Why is a research question so important?

Once you have decided on a research topic, it is time to start to devise a research question. This is an important step in the process because this gives your study a clear focus, helps you to 'keep on track' and avoids unnecessary and unhelpful diversions. Thomas (2017) argues that research questions lie at the heart of research and, going back to the Metaphorical Tent, your research question fulfils the role of your tent poles. The tent is of a traditional style with strong, solid poles that need to be located firmly on the ground and held in place by guy ropes. The canvas is hung over the poles (see Figure 5.1), which provide a robust framework to support the whole of the tent, keeping it erect and secure; this is especially important in case of bad weather. During a research study, this bad weather can take the form of many things that are not always expected (for example, personal difficulties, illness) because there is often no weather forecast! Having a clear research question helps you keep the project on track and moving forward.

Figure 5.1: The tent poles

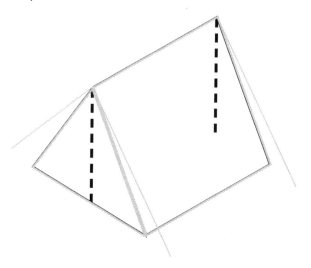

How to move from a topic to a research question

Moving from a topic to a research question is the next step in making progress towards your dissertation. Having found a topic you are interested in, you now need to move on to devise a research question (or questions). In qualitative research, the term research question is often used instead of **hypothesis** and it is useful at this point to explain the difference between these two terms. A hypothesis is defined by Kalaian and Kasim (2008: 731) as 'a specific, clear, and testable proposition or predictive statement about the possible outcome of a scientific research study'. It is a term that is usually applied to a quantitative study and sets out what the researcher is anticipating they will find. The study is then all about testing the hypothesis to find out if it is correct or not. By contrast, a research question is a term that is usually applied to qualitative research, and while many see it in terms of something to be answered, others see it as something to be explored (for example, Largan and Morris, 2019). Bearing in mind that in qualitative research there are usually no single clear-cut answers, the approach taken here is that a research question is better seen as something to explore. In this book the term research question is used in preference to hypothesis because the focus is on qualitative research.

Hypothesis – anticipates what you think you will find, is something to be tested and usually applies to quantitative research.

Research question – doesn't demand a single answer, is something to explore and usually applies to qualitative research.

Before we examine how to start writing a research question, we need to ask another question – do you need to devise a research question or research questions? My own preference here is to think of a single overarching question that you can then break down into a small number of sub-questions. Others prefer to have an aim for a research project with a number of research questions to explore. We discuss this later in this chapter.

In order to start writing a research question, we need to go back to the issue of curiosity (see Chapter 2). Here is a list of questions that can help you to make some initial progress when it comes to writing your research question. In relation to your topic area:

- What makes you curious?
- What do you want to investigate more closely?
- Which particular aspects do you want to find out more about?
- What sparks your interest in this?
- What has surprised you so far?
- What have you found to be unusual and unexpected?
- What have you expected to find, but haven't so far?

Thinking about questions like these can start to trigger ideas for a research question.

 Try making some notes under each of these questions in your research journal. Later, you might want to write about how you devised your research question in your dissertation, so having a record will be a very helpful time saver.

RAJESH

I'm starting to think about my research question, and I know I'm curious about the role of music and mental wellbeing. I'm particularly interested in how music can alleviate stress and, for now, I think this is an important aspect of my study. I've started to read about some of the different ways music can help people and have come across music as a particular therapy (called music therapy) that can be effective in addressing a wide range of mental health issues. Sounds really interesting. I want to look into this more and see what this could offer. I need to find out what its theoretical underpinnings are too. I think I need to build this into my research question, so, at the moment my overarching question could be something like 'How might music alleviate stress?'

What makes a good research question?

Research questions can come in all shapes and sizes and writing them can take some time. Many of my own students say that they find this difficult, but that spending some time on it is time well spent. Good research questions have some clear characteristics (see Figure 5.2) and they are as follows:

- open – they demand more than a yes/no answer and prompt a detailed response where both sides of an argument can be presented;
- clear – their language is concise and unambiguous, and they are invariably relatively short;
- focused – their wording is sharp and to the point, prompting a targeted study;
- achievable – they are not too ambitious or overcomplicated and make the whole project feel doable;
- detailed – they open up the possibility for analysis and are not simple or straightforward;
- not leading – they do not predict any results and could reach a range of different findings and recommendations;
- exploratory – they open up a range of areas for examination.

Figure 5.2: A good research question

By contrast, weak research questions are often:

- closed – answerable with yes or no;
- long – making it too easy to get lost within them;
- too wordy – making them difficult to follow and generally unclear;
- too broad – they make a small-scale study difficult and unmanageable;
- leading – showing (even predicting) what the researcher thinks they will find;
- two or more questions in one – so probably too big for a small-scale study and potentially confusing;
- explanatory – leading to work that is too descriptive.

Open questions (see Figure 5.3) cannot be answered with a simple yes or no and tend to start with words like:

what   where   when   how   why

They offer lots of scope for exploration.

Closed questions often start with the word 'do' and generally are best avoided.

Figure 5.3: Open questions

Use open questions when writing your research question and sub-questions.

EMMA

I'm trying to write my research question and I'm finding it much more difficult than I thought! So I'm going to make some notes in a table and write down the strengths and weaknesses of each them to see if I can make some progress.

Emma's notes are shown in Table 5.1.

Good research questions are often made up of a single, overarching question that captures the aspect of the topic you are curious about. This is then broken down into a small number of sub-questions (two to four) that will help you to examine some of the detail. In Table 5.1, we can see Emma's first attempts at writing a research question for her project on young people and reoffending. The strongest question seems to be the final one, although it could still be too broad. However, if we accept this at the moment as her overarching question, what might her sub-questions look like?

Table 5.1: Emma's possible research questions

Possible research question	Strengths	Weaknesses
Do people reoffend?	Focused on the topic	Closed – demands a yes or no answer
Do people reoffend too often?	Relevant to the topic	Closed and leading – seems to suggest they probably do
How often do people reoffend?	Relevant to the topic	More suitable for a quantitative study
Do young people enjoy offending and what makes them want to do it?	Relevant to the topic	Also leading and really two questions in one
What makes people reoffend?	Open and leaves scope for exploration	Could be too broad
What factors affect people who reoffend?	Open and invites a discussion of possible reasons why young people reoffend	Could still be too broad

Emma's overarching research question:
• What factors affect people who reoffend?

Possible sub-questions:
• When do people start offending?
• What makes them start offending?
• What makes them want to reoffend?

All of these questions are open and can give lots of scope for exploration in a qualitative desk-based study. The final sub-question keeps the study open and gives the opportunity to show that young people might be happy with their reoffending behaviour. If Emma is on an applied degree, such as youth work or social work, she might also want to consider having a final question that can lead her neatly into the conclusions and recommendations section of her dissertation. Her final sub-question could then be:

• What support might some people need to help them stop reoffending?

How do you write a good research question?

Writing a good research question often involves a process of writing down initial ideas and amending them. So, you shouldn't expect to be able to do this 'in one sitting' and it can take some time. Be ready to amend and adjust your ideas, and to rework your question and sub-questions. Taking some time to do this will be worth it and it's good to see it as time invested in your dissertation. Remember that your Metaphorical Tent really needs strong tent poles to make it robust and durable. Having strong research questions will definitely be very advantageous in the long run. Looking back to Emma's overarching question, it's possible that it is still too broad. Chapter 2 gives some ideas on how she might be able to narrow it down further. For example, she might decide to focus on a particular age group or a geographical locality.

Discussing your research questions with someone you trust is a good strategy. This could be your module tutor, your supervisor or a fellow student. Talking about things and, in particular, explaining them to someone else can really help you to develop your thinking. However, this is your research, so don't expect someone to tell you what to do – in fact, I could go a step further and say don't let someone tell you what to do! If you do, the danger is that your study becomes someone else's, and you can easily slip into researching their interests rather than yours. This might seem okay to start with, but later on your interest in the project might reduce and finishing it could then become difficult.

If you are struggling to devise your research question, do speak to your supervisor. They won't tell you what to do, so do be sure to draft out some possibilities beforehand that you can take to your discussion. That way you will have a good starting point.

Criteria for assessing a research question

At some point in the process of devising your research question, you will need to try and assess its quality. McCoombes (2020) sets out six key points that you can use in order to do this:

1. Focused – does it seek to explore a single issue or problem?
2. Researchable – will it enable you to carry out your research using desk-based resources and will it offer enough data for subsequent analysis?
3. Feasible – does it make your study doable within the time you have, bearing in mind any constraints you might experience that you can predict at the moment?
4. Specific – will it help you to produce some thorough work?
5. Complex – is it too simple and lacking in enough depth and breadth to give you enough material for your dissertation?
6. Relevant – is the connection with your degree subject clear?

If you can answer each of these positively, it is likely that your research question is fit for purpose. If not, you may well need to make some adjustments.

SAM

I've been thinking a lot about my research question and know it's really important to try and get it right. I suppose what I'm really interested in is the range of issues refugees seem to face. Mum has often spoken about people she knows who have experienced some real difficulties in various areas and I really want to explore some of these. I'm trying to work out if my question is suitable, so I'm going to try using McCoombes' six criteria to assess it and write notes under each of the headings. At the moment, my research question is 'What issues do refugees experience?'

1. Focused – it is focused on refugees, but I feel it could be too broad. It also assumes that refugees do have issues and difficulties.
2. Researchable – I'm feeling positive about this and it seems there are some relevant data resources and literature.
3. Feasible – I'm really not sure about this as the study seems too big, but at the moment the constraints seem small.
4. Specific – this is good and I feel happy about it. I know I'm really interested in this, which is good for my motivation.
5. Complex – everything seems very complex, maybe too complex?
6. Relevant – all good.

I'm going to arrange to see my supervisor to discuss things further and see if I can narrow my question down.

Can a research question be changed?

Many students assume that once a research question is written into a proposal (see Chapter 4) it cannot be changed. This is understandable, particularly if the proposal has been through an ethical review; but this is generally not the case. All researchers need to be mindful of the possibilities of bias and to be careful to be open-minded in their approach. Research that involves only looking for specific things or simply seeing what we want to see will not be robust when it is scrutinised for the purposes of assessment.

This is particularly the case in qualitative research. As discussed previously, a qualitative study is structured around a research question rather than a hypothesis. This research question is seen as something to explore where you may not find what you expect to find. In fact, qualitative research that unearths some surprising data is often more interesting, so to enable this, your research question needs to be sufficiently flexible that you can adapt it in relation to the literature you read and the data you collect. This is a reminder of the Research Triangle that we discussed in Chapter 1.

However, it will probably not be possible to change your research question completely. Your research proposal (see Chapter 4) may have been given clearance by an ethics committee, so if you change it substantially, it would have to go back to the committee for further consideration. This would be time–consuming and impractical in relation to the deadline for the submission of your dissertation.

A final word about your research question

A research question is pivotal to any study because, like the tent poles, it offers a supporting structure for the whole of your dissertation. Most dissertations are divided into sections and Table 5.2 summarises the importance of your research question in relation to each of these.

Table 5.2: The importance of your research question

Section of dissertation	Role of research question
Introduction	Explains clearly the focus of your study and offers a framework for the whole piece
Literature review	What has been published already in relation to my research question?
Methodology	How did I carry out my study to explore my research question?
Data analysis	What have I found out in relation to my research question?
Conclusions and recommendations	What conclusions have I reached in relation to my research question?

Table 5.2 demonstrates the importance of your research question in every aspect of your study. Remember that in a qualitative study it can (and indeed should) be amended in the light of what you discover.

SUMMARY

Writing a strong initial research question with sub-questions should put you in a good position to start carrying out your study confidently. But don't forget, you will probably amend them as your knowledge and understanding of your topic builds and your interests become sharpened. As the book progresses, we will see how Sam, Rajesh and Emma amend their research questions in the light of their progress. A study that has exactly the same research questions when it is complete as it had at the beginning could be said to be too predictable and even biased in its approach. Your research question will form an important part of the introduction to your dissertation and this is the focus of the next chapter.

Further reading

- O'Leary (2018) is a short book dedicated to the practicalities of devising research questions. It is full of practical steps and tips.
- White (2017) is another whole book devoted to developing research questions and is much more detailed. Chapters 1 and 2 give some very helpful strategies and techniques for this whole area.

6

Context, background and introduction

> In this chapter we will:
>
> ☐ develop an overview of a dissertation as a whole;
>
> ☐ discuss each aspect of writing an introduction to a dissertation;
>
> ☐ consider what motivates you in relation to your research project;
>
> ☐ examine the rationale for your study and its relevance;
>
> ☐ discuss the importance of considering the background to your study and issues of context;
>
> ☐ revisit your research question in order to refine it if necessary.

We now start to pay more attention to writing a dissertation, as well as keeping a close eye on the research process. In Chapter 3 we discussed the role of writing in relation to critical thinking; we write in order to understand rather than because we understand things already. This points to the likely need to draft and even redraft parts of your dissertation over a period of time in order to develop your understanding of the topic. Although this will take time, it will be worth it as it will help you to submit a dissertation that you can be proud of.

What does a whole dissertation look like?

A dissertation is probably the longest piece of work you will be asked to submit while studying at university. Some universities deliberately use the term independent study instead of dissertation, which gives a clear indication of what it is – something you do independently. This means you will need to manage your time well (see Chapter 14). However, this does not mean that you are engaged in any kind of 'yoyo' ('you're on your own') learning. You will be supported by a supervisor and building a good relationship with them will be key to your success (see Chapter 13). Don't forget those around you too who will also be able to support you, including friends, family and your fellow students. At times like this most of us need all the support we can get!

Many universities operate a clear system of asking students to write a certain number of words (or equivalent) to gain a specific amount of academic credits;

often, this is 4,000 words per 20 credits. Most dissertations attract 40 or even 60 credits, and some universities give students the choice of the size of their dissertation module offering these two options – and others. The word count you need to work to could potentially be between 8,000 and 12,000 words. Greetham (2019: 3) usefully discusses the difference between an essay and a dissertation, pointing out that the most obvious one is length. However, he also argues that this results in the need to 'analyse more extensively a larger body of material, critically evaluating it using more detailed and subtle arguments'.

 Always check the number of credits attached to your dissertation and the number of words you need to write. If in doubt, ask your supervisor, course leader or programme director.

Many students find it helpful to break a dissertation down by applying a clear structure. Often you will find this in your dissertation handbook or project guidance. Adding a word count to each of the sections can help you to see what you need to do more clearly and can also make everything appear more achievable. As an example, I often speak to my own students about using the following as a general framework for an 8,000-word project (see Table 6.1).

Table 6.1: Word counts

Introduction	1,000 words
Literature review	2,000 words
Methodology	2,000 words
Data analysis and discussion	2,000 words
Conclusions	1,000 words

Using a framework like this will help you to write a balanced dissertation. By this I mean a dissertation that will help you to meet all the relevant assessment criteria; doing this means you are more likely to achieve a high mark. Writing an unbalanced dissertation is likely to mean a lower mark because you won't score highly against all of the criteria; the impact of this could well be a lower mark overall.

 Universities stipulate many different requirements for students undertaking dissertations. The framework outlined in this section is meant for general guidance only and you should always check your university's own requirements to be on the safe side.

Many of my own students find writing some sections of a dissertation much more difficult than others and some common examples are presented in Table 6.2.

Table 6.2: Writing different sections of a dissertation

Introduction	Generally fine but difficult to write at the beginning of the research process. Often easier to write later, but can be counterintuitive, especially if you like to write things from start to finish.
Literature review	Often a longer section and it can be easy to 'get carried away' and write too much, especially if you are an avid reader. Difficult to keep to the word count.
Methodology	Often the most difficult section to write, mainly because you need to show good understanding of challenging abstract terminology. Tempting to write less and to give more words to other sections that might be easier.
Data analysis and discussion	The most difficult aspect can be making sure that this is an analysis and not just a description. Can be tempting to include everything, especially if you have interesting data and then write too much.
Conclusions	Generally fine and best written towards the end of the research process. Need to be sure to keep enough words for it, otherwise your work will end too abruptly, and the reader may feel that they have been left 'hanging' and wanting more.

In a quantitative study, data analysis and discussion are usually in separate sections: data analysis followed by discussion. Some supervisors prefer this even when you are doing a qualitative study, so be sure to find out and follow the advice given.

As well as understanding their own university's requirements, many students I work with also like to be able to see examples of dissertations students have completed before, because it is a different piece of work, and one they probably haven't done before. Some universities facilitate this by posting examples on their websites, while others make them accessible through the library; it is worth checking out what your own university offers.

It is great to see examples of dissertations, but please bear the following things in mind if you read them. You may not know what mark they received; the likelihood is the mark was high because universities want to showcase the best work of their students. If you are looking at a dissertation from another university, remember their assessment criteria might be very different from those of your own university, so this work might get a lower, or higher, mark if it were submitted to your university. In my experience, looking at examples can have two opposite effects: it might make you feel 'That's great, I can definitely do this!' or 'You know what, I thought I couldn't do this and now I know I can't!' So always read them with caution and be kind to yourself!

What does an introduction to a dissertation look like?

Saunders et al (2019) argue that a good introduction gives the reader a clear idea of the central issue of concern and why you feel it warrants closer examination. We now move on to examine in some detail what an introduction to a dissertation will usually contain. This forms the entrance to your Metaphorical Tent (see Figure 6.1) and is the way into what lies inside.

Figure 6.1: The entrance to the Metaphorical Tent

View from the front

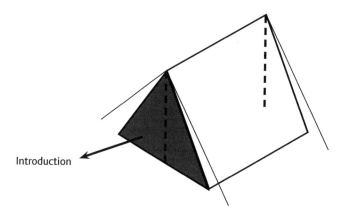

Using the framework in Table 6.1, if you are submitting a dissertation of 8,000 words, the introduction needs to be around 1,000 words long. It will probably need to cover the following areas:

- your motivation and why you are interested in your chosen topic;
- the rationale for your study;
- some relevant background information;
- the context of your study;
- the relevance of your study;
- your research question;
- a summary of what comes next, section by section.

We will now explore each of these in turn. You might write them in this order or not, it doesn't matter. Studying independently means the choice is ultimately yours but discussing each of them should mean that you are 'covering the bases', which will make your introduction strong and will provide a great 'launch pad' for your whole dissertation.

An introduction is the first chapter or section of a dissertation – you need to capture the reader's interest and draw them in. Make it sound like something they want to read!

Motivation

In Chapter 2 we saw the importance of choosing a topic that you are interested in to enable you to maintain a high level of motivation and reach the 'finish line'. In an introduction it is good to reserve a small amount of space to reflect on your own motivation for your project, including where your initial interest came from. If relevant, this might also include a related interest you have in a particular career area or postgraduate course for the future. Discussing your motivation means that you will make your own voice heard in your work, an important aspect of positionality (see Chapter 3) in qualitative research. This is another way of engaging with the reader and draws them into your work as they get to know a bit more about you.

Rationale

The word rationale means the fundamental reasons why we do something, in this case the reasons you are doing this research study. So, this is the place for discussing why you are doing this particular study and why you feel it is important. Here you can introduce your topic and discuss how you narrowed it down to reach your chosen focus (see Chapter 2), giving reasons for your choice. You might also include definitions of some key terms that the reader will need to understand in order to follow your main arguments.

 Remember to keep asking yourself the question 'Why?' This will help you to justify your arguments at every point.

EMMA

I've been doing a lot of background reading and I'm surprised by the large numbers of people who reoffend. It's made me think about why I want to do my project and why this whole area is important to me. I can see there is a real lack of support for offenders, especially young offenders, and feel if at all possible people should have more of an opportunity to turn their lives around in order to improve everyone's lives and society as a whole. This is an area that I feel passionate about and may even be something I want to build my future career in. I know I want to do something where I can make a difference and this could be one way of making that happen.

Background and context

Having introduced the topic, you will also need to give some background detail to your chosen topic and focus. Often this will include reasons why this area is timely and important. Here you might refer to a current debate, a relevant piece of news, a published report or items of published literature. It could also include looking back on how this area has become more important during recent years and, depending on your area of interest, it might also raise an issue or problem that you are seeking to explore in more depth. You could also point to a range of tentative conclusions that could be reached depending on the insights gained from your research.

RAJESH

I'm really enjoying doing my dissertation at the moment. I'm delving deeper into the whole area of the influence of music on mental wellbeing. I've recently read some interesting insights on a range of websites on how music can help people cope with a wide range of different issues. I've decided to focus this study on the way music can alleviate stress. I'm interested in exploring postgraduate courses in music and wellbeing and in the future I'm thinking about working in a community setting supporting people through music.

In discussing the background detail, you can also refer to the context for your research. For example, is your study based on a particular geographical area or region? Which particular communities are you investigating (for example, male or female, particular ethnic or age groups) and is there a particular time period that you are looking at? And so on (see Chapter 2).

Relevance

This is the place for showcasing the relevance of your research and gives the reader some clear reasons to read the whole piece of work. It could include things like:

- it helps to solve a practical or theoretical problem;
- it addresses a gap in knowledge;
- it builds on what is known already;
- it points to some new understandings or insights into your chosen area.

SAM

The news is often full of information about the experiences of refugees. There always seem to be people who have to flee their home country for some reason, often to escape things like war, conflict and persecution. I've read newspaper articles recently about migrants trying to enter the UK by crossing the Channel in dinghies and how they have sometimes been turned back. Some have died trying to cross the Channel, which is terrible. That could have been me and my mum. This is such an important area that really needs some urgent action.

At this point you might want to include a short pen picture of your research by way of a summary. This is probably a short paragraph describing what you did, and the data resources you used. Here you could also introduce your reasons for doing a desk-based study.

Some parts of your dissertation will need to be written in the past tense. It's good to do this as you go along if you can, as it can save you lots of time later on. To help you, imagine your study is complete and you are reading it in a year's time.

Your research question

This was the focus of Chapter 5 and it needs to be included at some point in your introduction. Bearing in mind that it supports the whole of your study, it is good to make it prominent and easy to find, for example by using a clear sub-heading. Be sure to include your overarching question and your sub-questions. As your study progresses, you may well need to amend and refine these in the light of your literature review and the data you collect. This is common in a qualitative study, and you shouldn't be afraid to do this more than once. This shows that your introduction could well be one of the last sections of your dissertation that you finalise.

Don't forget to go back to your research proposal; it is a working document and will remind you of some key things, such as your research question. But, resist the temptation to copy and paste as you might plagiarise yourself.

Summary of what comes next

Your introduction should finish with a summary of what comes next. This acts as an important signpost for the reader and means that your introduction has a nice neat ending. It is a simple summary of the forthcoming sections, with a pointer to your literature review in the next section of your dissertation.

Figure 6.2 shows each aspect of the introduction to a dissertation.

Figure 6.2: Aspects of an introduction

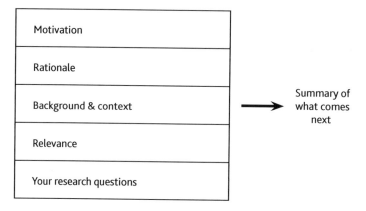

SUMMARY

In this chapter we have considered each aspect of the introduction to your dissertation. Sometimes it can be a difficult thing to start writing and if you find you are struggling, you can always start writing it later as things become clearer. The introduction forms the entrance to your Metaphorical Tent and points the way forward to the rest of your dissertation. In the next chapter we focus on selecting high-quality data resources for your project.

Further reading

- Becker (2015) provides some very helpful advice on writing an introduction to a dissertation, including when it might be written and what to include.

7

Selecting high-quality data resources

In this chapter we will:

☐ discuss how to use the internet to find data resources;

☐ consider and explore a wide range of different types of resources that can be used effectively in qualitative desk-based research – the first side panel of the Metaphorical Tent;

☐ become aware of some of the challenges in selecting data resources;

☐ discuss how to identify appropriate, high-quality data and develop some criteria for data selection;

☐ discuss the term **triangulation** in research;

☐ consider the issue of sample size.

Having chosen a topic for your study, devised an initial research question and written your proposal, it is now time to start to look in detail at where you will get your data from. Of course, you will have presented some initial ideas on this as part of your proposal and it is now time to delve deeper to make some key decisions. By now you will be able to see that your choice of data resources needs to be closely guided by your research question. Doing this means you are beginning to engage with the iterative research process as illustrated by the Research Triangle in Chapter 1.

The data resources you select make up the first side panel of your Metaphorical Tent (see Figure 7.1). There are vast amounts of easily accessible data that you could use very effectively in order to write a robust, insightful and engaging dissertation. The data you select really can bring a whole study to life, particularly as you give a voice to people who otherwise may well not be heard. Now is the time to think about a key question: 'What will I use as my data?' We move on to explore a range of data resources, most of which are accessible via the internet and will help you to respond to this question. Many of these resources could be used as a good basis for analysis and examination in relation to existing published literature. Although the process of data analysis might seem a long way ahead at the moment, it is well worth thinking about how you will analyse your data (see Chapter 11), as this can affect the data you choose. In essence, you need to be

Figure 7.1: The first side panel of the Metaphorical Tent

View from the back

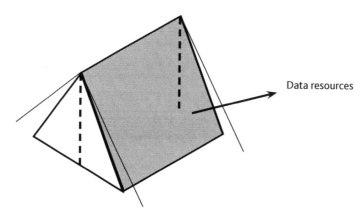

Data resources

sure that you can analyse your data effectively and relatively easily on a practical level and in sufficient depth.

When writing this section, I had to make a decision about the amount of detail to include here. On one level, a whole book could be written on this area alone and perhaps one will be in the not-too-distant future. But that is not the purpose of this book, so here, detail is not offered. Instead, each section includes examples of studies carried out using the resource in question with references to enable you to read more about them if you wish to do so. You may well also find it helpful to refer to Largan and Morris (2019) and Tight (2019), which both contain much more detail on these data resources than is possible to include here.

The examples included show how it is possible to use a particular type of data resource in academic research projects. The outcomes of these projects have all been published in peer-reviewed academic journals and are not meant to represent the kind of research project that an undergraduate student might do, so please don't be put off when you read them. However, many of them include a discussion of the strengths and weaknesses in the approach taken, which could be useful when you write the methodology section of your dissertation (see Chapter 9). In addition, they often explore how the data was coded, analysed and interpreted, which could offer you some helpful pointers when you do this in your own research project (see Chapter 11).

 These studies clearly confirm that you could use a wide range of data resources when carrying out a study for your dissertation.

Supervisors and tutors always love to see references to primary sources in their students' work (see Chapter 1). In my experience, many students receive feedback comments like 'you need to refer to more academic journal articles' and 'your work relies too heavily on websites and textbooks'. Academic journal articles like the ones referred to in this chapter are all examples of primary sources, as the papers present work from research projects that have been published in academic journals. They will all look great in a reference list and, if they are relevant to your project, they are well worth delving into.

How to use the internet to find data resources

Chapter 7 of Largan and Morris (2019), 'Locating your data', provides a full and comprehensive critical consideration of how to find the data you need via the internet, which is well worth reading. Here a small number of key points are offered in summary:

- You may well have begun your search for data early on in the research process, as you began to think about your topic and in starting to refine this into a research question. You may have also started to find potential data resources as you began searching for literature and, in addition, you needed to give an indication of your data resources in your research proposal.
- Remember to be ethical in your search; this will be explored further in Chapter 10.
- Use search engines effectively by using key words to set the boundaries of your search. These will reduce the number of sources presented and increase their relevance to your study.
- Be sure to use credible websites, ones that can be easily identified, such as those ending with .ac or .gov. It is usually best to avoid websites containing lots of advertisements.

(Drawn from Largan and Morris, 2019)

It is worth remembering that as soon as you start looking at data resources, you start the process of data analysis (Bachman and Schutt, 2008). This is because you immediately start to filter the material you are looking at and are constantly learning more about its relevance. This is the early stage of data analysis and doing this at this point is completely understandable and even inevitable. Because you already have a key interest in your chosen area and have some knowledge about it, your thought processes are all geared up for this early kind of analysis. The thing to be aware of here is to keep an open mind and maintain your curiosity. This way you will see new things you haven't seen before and avoid making assumptions.

Data resources can be grouped into three areas – written, visual and audio – and we now explore each of these in turn.

Written

Bowen (2009) argues that material in written form can provide a wide range of possible data resources for a research project. Historians have for a long time been aware of the importance of analysing written documents to understand a range of phenomena. However, this has been much less prominent in the social sciences (Scott, 1990). Written resources have many advantages; for example, they can often be easily downloaded and saved for later coding purposes (see Chapter 11 on data analysis) and if they are in paper form, they can be scanned and saved. The possible disadvantages are that you may well need to spend quite a lot of time reading and inwardly digesting them. Here are some examples of written resources, with studies where they have been used.

Minutes of meetings

Anyone who wants to can access online the minutes of meetings held by many different kinds of organisations. In general, these organisations are public bodies or those that have their public accountability monitored by independent regulators. For example, you can gain easy access to minutes of meetings held in schools, colleges, universities (including your own), healthcare providers, prisons, government departments, charities, local authorities and banks. Minutes of annual general meetings (AGMs) and other types of meetings can also be found online relatively easily using an internet search engine.

> Abimbola et al (2016) '"The government cannot do it all alone": realist analysis of the minutes of community health committee meetings in Nigeria'

> This is a study of healthcare provision in Nigeria and how it could be more effectively organised in the future to promote improved support through wider community engagement. The data used were minutes from community health committee meetings.

It is easy to spend hours online looking through minutes of meetings. If you can, go through the agendas first to guide you to the most relevant sections and be sure to keep an eye on the time!

Entries in diaries and journals

Examples of diary entries and extracts from journals available online are plentiful and could form an insightful basis for a qualitative study. Examples of these are historical diaries of a range of people during the Second World War, much more recent ones from teenagers highlighting their varied lived experiences of adolescence, plus those written by a variety of people on almost any topic you can mention. Some of the recent ones are updated daily and are accessible immediately for others to read. Each of these could provide you with some fascinating data for a desk-based study and can be found easily by a straightforward internet search.

> Day and Thatcher (2009) '"I'm really embarrassed that you're going to read this ...": reflections on using diaries in qualitative research'
>
> This study used the diaries of participants to research the experiences of competitive trampolinists over a period of time. It examines the pros and cons of using handwritten diaries as a data resource and some of the ethical issues involved.

 Qualitative research involves gaining insights leading to thick descriptions from the interpretation of data. Diaries and journals are personal and can be potentially powerful resources for analysis. Prepare to be engrossed!

Clippings and articles from newspapers and magazines

The easy availability of online newspapers and magazines means that there are many potential data resources for a wide range of qualitative studies. The issues covered by this kind of data are almost endless and whichever topic you have chosen to focus on, it is likely that there will be some data available in newspapers and magazines. As Grant (2019: 38) points out, 'the media ... is not producing a neutral reporting of events'. Many articles, especially those published in newspapers, have political agendas and editorial bias. Comparing articles on the same topic in different sources could lead to some fruitful analysis. Here is an example.

> Faucher (2009) 'Fear and loathing in the news: a qualitative analysis of Canadian print news coverage of youthful offending in the twentieth century'
>
> This explores how young offenders are depicted in Canadian newsprint media. The data was drawn from a sample of 1,937 news items from three of Canada's largest daily newspapers. The stories were found often to be sensationalist in nature and communicated through a dominant narrative of fear.

If you are considering using newspapers and magazines as a data resource, do be sure to check your university library for access. If the particular resource is not available there, check your local library. Accessing these through a library means you won't have to pay to subscribe in order to view them, which can get very expensive. Scanning relevant articles and saving them to view later can be very helpful, especially when you want to interrogate them as part of the process of data analysis.

Letters

You can also find published letters online which can offer a good data resource for a qualitative study. People write letters in relation to a wide range of issues; examples range from historic letters sent to relatives during the First World War to those sent in the present day. Some of these are written to individuals, such as letters to adopted children from their birth mothers, and others are letters to self, for example, suicide notes and letters addressed to my 'mental illness'. Some letters (except historical ones) are anonymous to preserve confidentiality. Here is an example of a study that used letters as a data resource.

Harris (2002) 'The correspondence method as a data-gathering technique in qualitative enquiry'

In this study letters were used in a project about women and self-harm. There is a good exploration of the use of letters as data and the ways in which they can open up an area that would otherwise be very difficult to research. There is also a consideration of the weaknesses and dilemmas involved in this approach.

It is easy to dismiss letters as a potential data resource just because most people don't write many letters these days and we're simply not used to reading them. If you take a bit of time to look at some in a bit of detail, you will soon see that some letters could offer rich data for analysis. Examining a sequence of letters could offer some fascinating insights into people's experiences and lives.

Reports from organisations (including charities, national and local government)

Annual reports from many organisations are readily available online and could also provide some useful data for a qualitative research project. Often reports are available from a number of previous years and could be used for comparative purposes when tracking changes that have happened over a period of time. Here is an example that demonstrates how annual reports can be used effectively in other ways.

Adams and Harte (1998) 'The changing portrayal of the employment of women in British banks' and retail companies' annual reports'

Published some time ago, this paper offers an interesting historical examination of the annual reports of companies from the retail and banking sectors in relation to the disclosure of equal opportunities information about the employment of women. Reports dating back to 1935 were selected for analysis. The findings show that when annual reports are used alongside information from a social, political and economic perspective, they can add to our knowledge of women's employment as being influenced by class and patriarchal power.

Reading reports sounds boring and at times it might be. If you decide to use reports as your data resource, a good approach is to skim-read them first to find the relevant sections you need to read in more depth later on. If the reports are available as PDFs, remember to use the 'edit-find' function to save you lots of time. You might need to download them first and save them to enable this function.

Biographies and autobiographies

Published biographies and autobiographies offer a wealth of personal data for a qualitative study. There are literally hundreds, if not thousands, available, so choosing the most useful ones could be a challenging decision, especially if there are a number written on your chosen topic; you will inevitably find a lot to feed your interests and passions! Here again you will need to be guided closely by your research question. In the case of biographies, it will be important to consider who it was written by and what their agenda might have been when writing it. Here is an example of a research study where these have been used.

Lester (1989) 'Experience of parental loss and later suicide: data from published biographies'

In this study the biographies and autobiographies of 30 people who had committed suicide were explored. The findings were that 16 of them showed they had experienced bereavement in childhood with most having lost a father rather than a mother. In addition, 14 of the 16 had experienced this loss between the ages of six and 14 years.

 Biographies can be compelling and very thought-provoking. Keeping a record of your thoughts and feelings in your research journal as you progress in your search for data resources will help you to critically evaluate your work later on.

SAM

I've been having great difficulty deciding on my data source. Everything is so interesting! And really quite emotional too. It's all making it very difficult to choose. I know I want to delve deep into my data and that I can't have too much of it, or I'll feel swamped. I've been finding lots of biographies of refugees and think these could be a great data resource. But how do I know that the quality will be good enough? I've also been looking at the United Nations High Commissioner for Refugees (UNHCR) website where they describe some biographies and choosing from these feels much more secure than just choosing ones I'm interested in. I've found two that are really moving and detailed – but now I can't decide. Is one going to be enough? Do I need more than one for comparison? I'm going to email my supervisor to see if we can talk it through.

Blogs, social media postings and websites

Of course, written material is not only available on paper. More recent examples of data resources include blogs and postings on various social media sites such as Facebook and Twitter, plus websites. In their discussion of using blogs in research, Hookway and Snee (2017) describe blogs as contemporary documents, offering rich, spontaneous descriptions of everyday life experiences.

Harricharan and Bhopal (2014) 'Using blogs in qualitative educational research: an exploration of method'

This paper explores the use of blogs in examining the experiences of international students adjusting to studying in the UK. It highlights the underuse of blogs as a data resource.

It is good to remember that, like other data resources, websites can be politically motivated and it is always worth bearing this in mind when deciding whether to select them or not. Of course, it could be that a comparison of two or more websites that take contrasting stances could lead to lots of interesting data for analysis and a very fruitful study. It is always good to keep an open mind when it comes to choosing data resources and to be practical. If you can't find a particular source easily, try an alternative. Where appropriate, some students choose to carry out their studies in their own universities via their websites because access to data (such as policies) is often much easier. This is known as opportunity sampling.

Visual

There are many different sources online offering a range of visual material that you could use as data for your research. Pauwels (2010: 550) argues that 'social scientists should take advantage of the wide sweep of data sources available in society'. You will no doubt be used to seeing a broad range of video material as you surf the internet, and it is well worth keeping an eye on things that grab your attention in relation to your dissertation topic. You may also find other visual data like photographs, pieces of artwork, maps and diagrams that stand out to you when you see them. There are many advantages in using visual data and, as Pauwels (2010: 550) argues, as well as giving us insights into the way society functions, they can also provide 'access to broader and more profound aspects of society'. However, he also points to some disadvantages in relation to using visual data, such as a lack of background and contextual knowledge along with potential copyright issues (see Chapter 10). Another important issue to bear in mind if you are thinking about using visual resources is quality. There is nothing worse than watching a poor recording and trying to decipher what is being said. This can be frustrating and very time-consuming. The same applies to examining poor-quality stills or photographs.

Videos and video logs (vlogs)

Following the development of relatively cheap and high-quality recording equipment, not least of which is the smartphone, we can all be film-makers. Of course, this does not mean that anyone can make an award-winning film, but it does mean that many people have become interested in recording aspects of their everyday lives and uploading them on the internet via sites like YouTube, Vevo, Videvo and many more. This has resulted in a vast array of videos and vlogs that you could use very effectively as data. A quick search online could well reveal a range that you could use as data resources related to your research question.

Giglietto et al (2012) 'The open laboratory: limits and possibilities of using Facebook, Twitter, and YouTube as a research data source'

This is a thorough literature review of studies carried out using these media and offers a wealth of references that you could look at. It highlights the advantages and disadvantages of these different approaches.

 Items on news websites can disappear very quickly and then be very difficult to find. To be on the safe side, it is well worth using your smartphone to record something while it is playing on your laptop or PC.

Films, drama and TV documentaries

Other visual material comes in the form of films, drama and TV documentaries. Many film and TV programmes dating back a considerable number of years can be accessed via archives like that of the British Film Institute (2020). Unfortunately, many early TV programmes and documentaries were either not recorded because they were only ever transmitted live, or their recordings were subsequently destroyed. This was often the case before the 1980s. In these circumstances, you might need to rely on clips or extracts that you can find on the internet rather than the whole programme.

> Stanley (2008) 'Celluloid angels: a research study of nurses in feature films 1900–2007'
>
> This paper explores the ways in which nurses have been portrayed in films during the period identified. They highlight how these portrayals have changed over time with more recent films showing nurses to be strong and self-confident unlike their earlier counterparts.

We all know how easy it is to see something online that we feel is important or useful. Without thinking we move on to something else and forget what we saw, close a window accidentally or 'lose' things when our computer does automatic updates. Of course, we can always trawl through our web history, but that can be very time-consuming. Copying and pasting a URL into a blank document when we see something that we think is going to be important and saving it can be a really helpful and time-saving habit to develop.

EMMA

My interest in reoffending among young people is really continuing to develop. I'd like to talk to young offenders directly about this, but I can see that a number of ethical issues would prevent this. So, as well as examining websites of relevant charities, I'm going to look for TV documentaries where this issue has been discussed. Today I was browsing through a range of possibilities online and found some potentially interesting data where reoffenders share their stories. Some of these could offer some great scope for analysis in my dissertation.

Visual stills

Still visual material can also be used as a data resource in qualitative research and can range from photographs, pieces of artwork, illustrations, advertising posters, as well as material on websites such as Pinterest. There are several archives where these can be found, for example, the Advertising Archives (nd) and Historic England (2020).

> Pauwels (2008) 'Taking and using: ethical issues of photographs for research purposes'
>
> This paper examines a range of ethical issues in using photographs in research (see Chapter 10). It points to the many difficulties in protecting the **anonymity** and privacy of research participants and the thorny issue of gaining **informed consent**.

We will consider the issue of informed consent in Chapter 10 on ethics. For now, it is good to remember that we shouldn't take anything for granted and that you will need to try and gain informed consent whenever possible. We certainly shouldn't slip into thinking that because someone has posted something online that they are automatically happy for us to analyse it as part of a research project.

Audio

Alongside the growth of sites like YouTube has been the development of podcasts and other types of audio recordings. Of course, people have listened to the radio for many more years than watching TV or film, so this medium can offer some historical perspectives too. Downloading audio recordings to your laptop or device can give you safe and immediate access for the length of your study, which is extremely helpful. Often a link to a website is provided that will give a transcript of the recording, which is again invaluable for data analysis.

> Kakade (2013) 'Credibility of radio programmes in the dissemination of agricultural information: a case study of Air Dharwad, Karnataka'
>
> This study explores the use of radio as a means of communicating with people in rural India where literacy levels are low. Radio is found to be a useful means of disseminating important scientific information about farming to people in isolated communities.

Many resources can be found in libraries and archives and are accessible via the internet using appropriate indices, such as British Library Sounds. If you want to use some of these but are having difficulties in finding those that are most useful for your project, be sure to ask your library staff who will be happy to help you.

RAJESH

My love of music is helping me see more of how it helps others deal with their anxiety issues as well as me. I've been doing some more searching for resources online and have found a series of podcasts on the different ways that music can help people with mental health issues. I'm going to listen to some of them to find out if this is the kind of data resource I want to use in my study. The great thing is the data is all there and really easy to access.

The challenges of deciding which data resources to use

For a range of reasons, it can be difficult to decide which data to use in desk-based research. This decision can be just as important as deciding who to interview or who to ask to complete a questionnaire in an empirical study. Some of these challenges are explored here.

Selecting your data resources is likely to feel like an important decision. You may well need to do this at what might feel like a pivotal point in your study; and you are probably right! You need to make this decision in order to move forward and until you do so, your progress may well be hindered; as time goes on, you could even begin to feel stuck. Figure 7.2 illustrates this.

Figure 7.2: The pivotal point

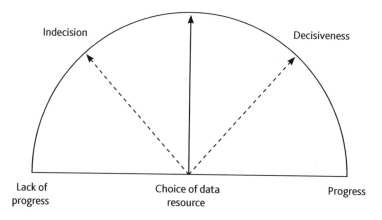

In my experience, reaching this point can affect different students in different ways. Some are ready to make a decision and take some big steps forward in their study. Others are more hesitant and can start to 'bury their heads in the sand' or even begin to panic; both are equally understandable but undesirable responses. A mistake that many students make at the point of deciding on their data resources is to procrastinate and put it off until later. In the meantime, they fill their time with reading more literature (or for the avid readers out there, this can be *even more* literature) to help them decide. Reading relevant literature is clearly not a bad thing per se and this approach might work, or it might not. You might read more, find a focus and start to make progress. Or you might read more and become confused or side-tracked, which will hold you back. You might even read in the never-ending search for that 'perfect' piece of literature, which could result in feeling completely swamped. It is always worth remembering that procrastination is 'the thief of time' (see Chapter 14); in the end, the time available for writing a dissertation simply runs out.

Another major reason why students 'grind to a halt' at the point of selecting their data resources is because they are nervous about making a mistake that they might regret later on. This is completely understandable. However, while this is possible, it is well worth remembering three things:

- First, it is very rare for any research project to go completely according to plan. If you ultimately feel you chose the wrong data, or could have selected better data, you won't be alone.
- Second, a strong dissertation will probably include a critical evaluation of the research process, including what you could have done differently and why. So, if you feel you could or should have selected different resources, you will have quite a lot to reflect on in your work and write about, which is a positive thing.
- Third, your supervisor is there to help you to make good decisions. A good supervisor won't tell you what to do but will be happy to hear about the various resources you are looking at and this should help you to decide, as well as offering you some welcome reassurance.

Table 7.1 contains some common reasons why students find it challenging to select their data sources, with some possible remedies.

 If you are having difficulties selecting your data resource, talk to your supervisor as soon as you can. Send them a friendly email (but not too casual!) outlining what you would like to talk about so they can think about how they can support you.

How to identify appropriate, high-quality data

As we have seen, there is a wealth of qualitative data available. Largan and Morris (2019: 18) argue that 'all forms of documentary evidence exist as possible sources of data' (including such things as photographs, videos and social media posts) and can be used in a research project. However, this begs the question as to whether

Table 7.1: Difficulties in selecting data resources and possible remedies

Challenges	Remedies
It feels scary and is making me anxious because it is a really important decision	Talk to people who are there to support you (for example, staff in wellbeing and your personal tutor)
I'm worried about getting stuck and everyone else seems to be making much more progress than me	Try not to compare yourself with others; in the end it's only what *you* do that really counts
I really want a good mark and if I choose the wrong data, I won't get one	Academic marking criteria usually ask you to critically evaluate how you selected your data, and do not give you marks based on the data itself. This means you will have a lot to write about in the relevant section of your dissertation.
I can't select my data resources because I haven't read enough literature	Many people (including me!) often feel they haven't read enough, but don't let this stop you. You will continue to read throughout your project. But equally, don't kid yourself if you know you haven't read very much!

all of this is useable as a resource for a research project and it seems right to treat all possible data resources with caution for the following four reasons.

First – they may be of poor quality. If data is unclear (for example, it cannot be seen or heard well) or too brief it may not have the potential to give us new insights.

Second – they will no doubt have been created for different purposes and not for research. While lots of data may well be interesting, it will not always be relevant.

Third – they may be unrelated to research and any particular research questions you are wanting to explore.

Fourth – they will have been created without any researcher involvement. Other types of qualitative data that people gather, such as recordings of interviews and focus groups, have been made with clear research questions in mind that have been written by the researcher. In addition, questions that participants are asked have also been carefully formulated in order to gain insights into the research question.

When selecting data resources online, you will need to use some clear criteria to guide you and here my ISAACC model (as illustrated in Figure 7.3) could help. At its heart lies a questioning approach to every part of the data selection process:

- *Insights* – you need to be clear about the insights the data could bring to your research question. This shows whether or not the data is relevant and fit for purpose. This is an absolutely central concern, because if the answer is 'Well, it's very interesting, but nothing really', the data in question could be a very unwelcome diversion at this point when time is so precious. You could potentially spend a lot of time analysing something that you decide isn't relevant after all.

You need to pose the question 'How does this relate to my research project?' at each step of the data selection process.

- *Selective* – be very choosy when it comes to your data resources because this helps you to guard against the real potential for data overload. With a vast amount of data available, you will need to focus in on the data that is most useful to your study. You may find you need to be ruthless in discarding, and even ignoring, resources at various points.

  Posing the question 'Is the data vital, important, possibly relevant or unimportant in relation to my study?' will be necessary.

- *Assumptions* – make them at your peril! Be sure to take a questioning approach and interrogate everything. Largan and Morris (2019: 167) go even further and encourage us to be 'sceptical' as we go through this process, implying that we need to be convinced of the value of the data resource.

  Pose questions such as 'Is the data credible?', 'Is it authentic?', 'Can it be trusted?' and 'Is it in any way typical in relation to other data that is available?' All these questions need a positive response to ensure the data is definitely worth using.

- *Ask more questions* – basic ones like 'Who, what, when, where and how?'

  For example, 'Who wrote or recorded the data and what kind of reputation do they have, if any?', 'When was it recorded and what was going on around that time?', 'What was the purpose of recording it, if any?', 'Where was it recorded?' and 'How was it received?'

- *Context* – if it is similar to that of your research project, the data is likely to be more useful. You need to beware of data from very different contexts (for example, from other parts of the world, from different demographics from those in your study, from people in very different situations) that cannot easily be applied to your study, as doing so could be misleading.

  Think about the context of the resource and ask 'How similar is it to mine?'

- *Clarity* – the data needs to be able to be understood.

  So, 'Is it legible, audible and comprehensible?'

  (Drawn from Scott, 1990; McCulloch and Richardson, 2000; Fitzgerald, 2007)

It is often useful to make a record of how you selected your data resources, so you can go back to it as and when necessary. You will also need to write about this process in the methodology section of your dissertation (see Chapter 9).

Figure 7.3: The ISAACC model

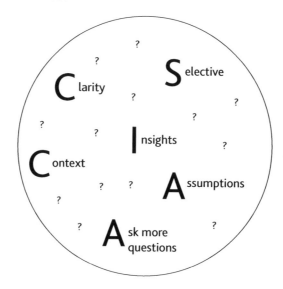

 Be sure to write about how you selected your data resources in your research journal. You may think you will remember this, but with everything else going on, you may well forget!

Triangulation

This is a term borrowed from surveying and is used in a metaphorical sense in social science research. The idea behind it is that examining something from more than one viewpoint is better than only examining it from one. The term triangulation implies three different viewpoints, but this is not necessarily the case and it could be more or fewer than three, but definitely more than one. Triangulation in research makes a study more robust and less open to criticism in relation to bias. When deciding on your data resources, it will be useful to consider how you will triangulate your study; this is known as data source triangulation. For example, you might want to use different sources to explore the same phenomenon; this could be a number of videos or podcasts, or a single video and a single podcast. Equally, you may decide to use a number of written online case studies or journal entries. Whatever you decide, it will be good to consider the different perspectives each could bring to your study.

Sample size

At some point you will need to decide on the size of your data sample. It is always worth remembering that you are using qualitative methods to gain some data to analyse in depth in order to interpret it, so you can then write some thick description (see Chapter 9). Qualitative research is not about making large claims that can be generalised across populations (see Chapter 9) and indeed, many quantitative studies would struggle to do this. So, a qualitative sample will inevitably be fairly small.

So how small is fairly small? This is the billion–dollar question! In some studies, a sample of one can be justified, for example if it is a deep exploration into the life and experiences of an individual. However, for the purposes of triangulation (see Chapter 9), more than one resource will be needed to carry out this exploration. For other studies a sample of four to six will often be enough to give material for comparative purposes. More than six for a qualitative dissertation can lead to two unwanted effects. The first is too much data which can be overwhelming, and the second is that you begin to 'hear' the same things again but from different people. In qualitative research this is referred to as 'data saturation'; this is the term used to assess whether or not there is sufficient data for a robust study (Hennink and Kaiser, 2019). In my own work with students I often advise a sample size of four to six, but when making this decision, always check with your supervisor. Remember quality and relevance are important too, as discussed in the previous section.

If you're in doubt about your sample size, be sure to discuss this with your supervisor who will guide you. They will also have a view – and they will be marking your work!

SUMMARY

In this chapter we have considered a range of issues related to finding and selecting qualitative data for your desk-based study. It is easy to feel overwhelmed by the amount of data resources available, and if you find this happening, be sure to go back and ask yourself what you are really interested in finding out. Remember too that your research questions are there to guide you. When you have made your selection, it will be time to move on to reviewing literature. You may well have started this already and in the next chapter we focus on this specifically.

Further reading

- Grant (2019) includes a wealth of information on using documents in social research. This includes many different sources that are available via the internet, including social media.
- Salmons (2019) offers an excellent short guide on a range of issues connected with accessing data via online sources.
- Thomas (2020) provides a short and very accessible introduction to getting your data from social media.

8

Literature review

Having considered a wide range of possible data resources, we now move on to the whole area of carrying out a literature review. This is a relatively large part of the research process and one where you can demonstrate your knowledge and understanding of published work on your topic area as well as your literature search skills. Doing your literature review will undoubtedly mean reading lots of material you will find interesting and making some key decisions along the way.

The role and purpose of a literature review

Having begun to select some high–quality data resources, it is now time to consider the role and purpose of a literature review in your desk–based study. Early on in the research process when you considered a range of topics for your study, you were encouraged to select something of interest to the academic community (see Chapter 2). This meant choosing an area that has been researched by academics already, resulting in a range and amount of published academic literature for you to read and critically evaluate. In addition, you were undoubtedly asked to identify some of the key areas of literature related to your topic in your research proposal. One word that is sometimes used to describe a literature review is a survey; this has the aim of providing an overview of current knowledge of your area of study. Doing a survey like this involves identifying relevant theories and models as well as any gaps in existing research. The purpose of a literature review then is to critically examine a range of publications linked to your study and it forms the second side panel of the Metaphorical Tent (see Figure 8.1).

Figure 8.1: The second side panel of the Metaphorical Tent

View from the front

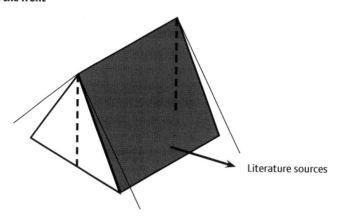

Literature sources

When trying to start a literature review, many students ask me questions like 'How do I know what to read in relation to my topic?' and 'Where do I start with knowing what to read?' This is often because topic areas can be large, with an amount of literature that can sometimes be daunting and even overwhelming. This is where your research question and sub-questions come back into the foreground – those tent poles that support the whole of your Metaphorical Tent (see Chapter 5). The answer to both of the questions posed by my students is to read what has been published already that relates to your research question. Devising your research question with its sub-questions means that you have already made some decisions about which aspect or aspects of your topic you are curious about, and these will give your study a sharper focus than simply looking at the topic as a whole. Overall, this should make the task of a literature review easier as your research question has helped you to start to refine your interest, and acts as a lens through which you can read about and examine your topic. Rather like the lens of a microscope, your research question helps you to gain a clear and precise view of some key aspects of your topic.

 Your research question guides you to what you should read and helps you to examine key aspects of your topic.

A literature review will perform a number of functions in relation to your topic (see Figure 8.2), including:

- Giving some more detailed background in relation to your study. We covered this in part in Chapter 6, but there is only so much background information you can, and indeed should, discuss in an introduction to a dissertation. Your literature review will probably give you the opportunity to add more.
- Giving you an opportunity to show the breadth and depth of your knowledge of a range of key aspects.
- Helping you to identify any gaps in current thinking and research.
- Giving you the opportunity to critically analyse, evaluate and synthesise relevant literature.
- Enabling you to show your understanding of how thinking has developed in this area over time.
- Showing your awareness of the range of arguments presented by academics who have done research in your chosen area.

Figure 8.2: Aspects of a literature review

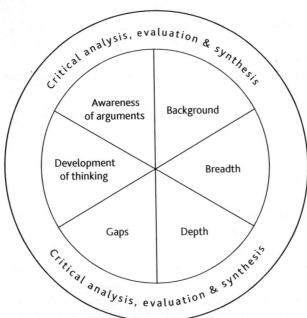

The difference between a literature review as a whole dissertation and a literature review as part of a dissertation

At this point it is useful to clarify the difference between a literature review as a whole dissertation as distinct from one that is part of a dissertation. In my experience, some students find this confusing. A literature review can be done as a piece of research in its own right; in this instance a literature review is a methodology in and of itself and forms the whole of a dissertation. It is a form of secondary research (see Chapter 1) and means that reviewing the literature makes up the whole dissertation. Aveyard (2019) gives an excellent framework for this and Hewitt-Taylor (2017: 1) also writes on this subject. She discusses the value of carrying out a literature review as a whole piece of research when she says 'Good quality reviews of existing literature, that provide a rigorously derived summary of what is and what is not currently known about a subject, and the strength of the evidence that exists, can … be very useful.' While a literature review as part of a desk-based study is clearly a smaller task, the same principles apply. Some of the words Hewitt-Taylor uses here are worth emphasising:

- good quality – all research needs to be of good quality if it is going to stand up to a university's assessment process and a literature review shouldn't be seen as any different in this respect;
- review – not simply a description of the literature that is available, but a critical appraisal;
- rigorously derived – this means that it is done in a careful, thorough and purposeful way;
- known and not known – it should point to gaps in knowledge as well as focusing on what we know already;
- strength of evidence – not all evidence is strong, and this implies the need for critique and robust evaluation.

Steps involved in a literature review

Doing a literature review as part of a dissertation often involves following a number of key steps, which are outlined here.

Step 1 – search for literature that is relevant to your research question. You will probably need to do this in a number of different ways, for example, using your own university library, reliable sources on the internet such as Google Scholar and appropriate databases giving access to journal articles and published research reports.

Step 2 – you will need to evaluate your sources. Some sources are more reliable than others and the reliable ones are the ones to focus on. To select appropriate literature, you will need to use the methods outlined previously and to avoid unreliable sources, particularly many internet sources. Be sure to avoid websites that just describe theories and approaches (for example, BusinessBalls, Mind Tools, Wikipedia) as these will affect your literature review adversely.

Step 3 – identify themes and debates within the relevant literature. This is a key step and prevents your review from becoming some kind of summary or description of what has been written. At this point you might want to start making some kind of visual map or a list of the range of arguments being made in relation to your research question. This can be very helpful when you need to decide on a structure for your review (Step 4) in order to start to write it up and it doesn't need to be complicated. For example, keeping a list of key words can be very helpful and you may well use this later on as part of the data analysis process.

Step 4 – decide on a structure. This can take a variety of forms and each has its relative strengths and weaknesses (see Table 8.1).

Step 5 – write the review.

Table 8.1: Different structures for a literature review

Type of structure	Strengths	Weaknesses
Chronological	Tracks the development of thinking in an area over a period of time and shows how ideas and theories have developed	Can be too descriptive and has the potential to be repetitive
Thematic	Identifies recurring themes in literature and can link well with a thematic approach to data analysis (see Chapter 11)	Could encourage you to find themes too quickly and then to make assumptions about your data
Methodological	Identifies research using particular methodologies (see Chapter 9) which can give a sharp focus	Means you might miss key literature that is derived using a different approach
Theoretical	Covers a range of important perspectives on a topic	Might be too broad and lack focus

The most common approach taken to a desk-based literature review is a thematic one. However, it is also possible, and can be quite valuable, to combine these different elements to carry out a robust review.

 TIP Don't forget to talk to staff in your university library, especially your subject librarian. They will be very happy to help you find a range of appropriate sources of literature for your study and to point you in the direction of things you might not have found.

Largan and Morris (2019: 189) offer some useful tips when they outline what a literature review is not:

- a list of sources;
- a list of things you have read with descriptions of the content;
- a personal interpretation of what you have read;
- some kind of extended essay.

Perhaps the most important point they make is that it is not a chance to show everything you have read. You will undoubtedly read more than there will be room for you to include in your review. This means that at some point you will need to select the most valuable sources you have found and focus on these. Making your selection could well mean not including some really interesting things that you will have read. This can be disappointing but is all part of the process.

Some academic journals publish literature reviews as articles. These are well worth looking for in relation to your topic as they can provide a summary of the kind of literature to look for in your review along with the references you will need. Most academic journals also publish book reviews regularly and this can be a great way of hearing about new publications.

 TIP **Look out for published literature reviews in relation to your topic. These can save you quite a lot of work and give some very useful signposts.**

Here is an example of a published literature review.

Snelson (2016) 'Qualitative and mixed methods social media research: a review of the literature'

This paper analysed 229 mixed methods studies to put together a literature review on the use of social media in research. It offers a whole variety of references to some of the studies which could be an invaluable source of primary literature for the literature review section of a dissertation.

Advice can vary in relation to when you should carry out a literature review, which can be confusing and frustrating. Many research methods lecturers and supervisors argue that it should be done (and even completed) early on in the research process. This is because it is seen as part of preparing to collect and analyse your data. This approach generally applies to quantitative research as it forms a key part of the process of developing a hypothesis that is then tested. However, the view often taken in qualitative research, and in this book, is that it is useful to collect some data first before carrying out the bulk of your literature review; hence the chapter on data resources comes before this one. This means that your own interpretation of the data isn't skewed by what you have read.

Reading about what others have found first can mean that we look for the same things in our data rather than offering our own interpretations. This is often because we understandably assume they know more about the topic than we do because they have researched it already. This means in turn that our study can become somewhat predictable as we find things that have already been identified by other researchers rather than focusing on what might be new and different.

However, this does not mean that we can completely leave working on a literature review until later; in fact, it probably means we do it as a more continuous process throughout the period of time we have. This is a reminder of the Research Triangle (see Chapter 1) where we engage in the iterative process of reviewing literature alongside our data (see Figure 8.3).

Figure 8.3: The Research Triangle – literature

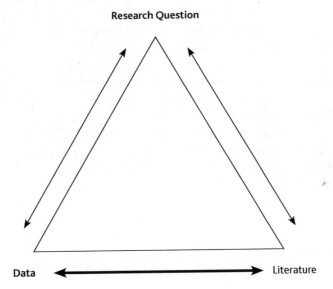

Characteristics of a strong literature review

In Chapter 1 we looked at primary, secondary and tertiary sources for a desk-based study. We return to this here in relation to sources of literature for a strong review.

Primary sources contain material that is original. This includes academic journal articles and reports that publish findings from primary research. Some academic books (for example, research monographs) also present findings from primary research and original scholarship written in a longer and more detailed form than is possible in an article for an academic journal. Research monographs can also be presented as part of a collection of chapters in an edited book. Here are some examples.

EXAMPLES OF GOOD PRIMARY SOURCES FOR:

Sam
Brownlie, S. (2020) *Discourses of Memory and Refugees: Exploring Facets*

A research monograph detailing a study of memory and refugees in the United Kingdom sheds light on an under-researched area, explores methodological issues and introduces 'facet methodology' to the field of memory studies. Provides a fascinating and well-constructed group of case studies.

Rajesh
Bonde, L.O. and Theorell, T. (eds) (2018) *Music and Public Health: A Nordic Perspective*

An edited collection of chapters in a book, presenting research studies from Denmark, Norway, Sweden and Finland. Discusses examples of the therapeutic and health-enhancing effects of music, showing the benefits of music in relieving physiological, psychological and socioemotional dysfunction.

Emma
Hazel, N. (2018) '"Now all I care about is my future". Supporting the shift: framework for the effective resettlement of young people leaving custody'

A report on a piece of research funded by the Big Lottery presenting a new framework for understanding the effective resettlement of young offenders.

Secondary sources describe, summarise and analyse primary sources. These include textbooks and other written material that review and evaluate original sources. Here are some examples.

EXAMPLES OF GOOD SECONDARY SOURCES FOR:

Sam
Jalonen, A. and Cilia la Corte, P. (2018) *A Practical Guide to Therapeutic Work with Asylum Seekers and Refugees*

A practical book written for a range of professionals including therapists, teachers, social workers, housing support workers and healthcare professionals. Described as an essential guide giving useful background information on the asylum seeker and refugee experience and guidance on how to provide them with excellent support.

Rajesh

Wheeler, B.L. (ed) (2018) *Music Therapy Handbook*

Provides a comprehensive overview of music therapy, from basic concepts to emerging clinical approaches. Experts review psychodynamic, humanistic, cognitive-behavioural and developmental foundations and describe major techniques.

Emma

Case, S. (2018) *Youth Justice: A Critical Introduction*

A comprehensive and critical introduction to youth justice in England and Wales. Offers a balanced evaluation of its development, rationale, nature and evidence base. Brings theory and practice together to explore definitions and explanations of youth offending and examines the responses to it that constitute youth justice.

Tertiary sources compile and organise mostly (although not exclusively) secondary sources to make them easier to find. These offer a key guide, especially when starting a literature review and include catalogues (such as the one for your university library), databases (like EBSCO and ProQuest) which can guide you to relevant academic journal articles, and those that particularly focus on finding abstracts (such as Educational Abstracts Online). A number of these will help Sam, Rajesh and Emma with their reviews.

A strong literature review shows breadth and depth of knowledge and understanding in relation to a topic. This is a reminder of Thompson's (2012) 'helicopter vision' that we covered in Chapter 3, which enables us to see the big picture and the detail. While on the surface this seems contradictory and difficult to achieve, here are some pointers, specifically as they relate to carrying out a literature review:

- Secondary sources often offer an excellent overview of topics and issues, and frequently show how ideas and theoretical concepts have changed over time. As such they are very useful sources for helping us to show breadth of understanding. Primary sources help us to 'drill down' into specific aspects of a topic as they tend to focus much more specifically on particular issues or questions with evidence from research. A strong literature review probably needs to draw on both types of sources.
- Gaining some breadth first is often valuable as this helps us to identify what we then need to focus on to get depth in a literature review. Although this is not a 'hard and fast' rule, it could be useful to read some textbooks first (or to go back to the textbooks you have read) and then delve into some journal articles, monographs or books that are presented as edited collections.
- When writing your review, it will not be possible to write in detail about everything you have read. In fact, you will need to make choices and leave

out some undoubtedly interesting things you have read because they do not relate directly to your research question or one of your sub-questions. This is always difficult, especially because you have a strong interest in your topic.

- At some point you will need to select a small number of key readings to focus on. These will be the sources that have the most, and the most interesting, things to say in relation to your research question. Examining these in detail will enable you to show depth of knowledge. You can then compare and contrast these with other authors to show breadth of knowledge as well.

 Even though you are doing a qualitative desk-based study, your literature review may well include some quantitative studies. These can be particularly relevant for background detail in relation to the context of your topic.

Like any other piece of academic work, writing a strong literature review involves presenting both sides (or more) of an argument and then putting forward a considered view of your own based on the evidence you have found. In qualitative desk-based research this is always best done using tentative language, as there are always multiple interpretations (see Chapter 9). Table 8.2 contains some examples to show the difference between language that is inappropriate and appropriate for a qualitative study.

Table 8.2: The language of a qualitative desk-based study

Inappropriate language	Appropriate language
It is obvious that …	It seems apparent that …
Evidence shows without doubt that …	Evidence suggests that …
It is definitely the case that …	It is generally thought that …
It is unmistakable that …	It is generally accepted that …
It is always the case that …	It is often asserted that …

What is the difference between analysis, evaluation, description and synthesis?

In my experience students often struggle with understanding the difference between analysis, evaluation and description in relation to writing a literature review and can also find the term synthesis difficult. Critical thinking (see Chapter 3) involves analysis and means being ready to question something, to examine it in detail in order to understand its component parts. This is different from a detailed description of something. For example, a detailed description of a research report will include what the researchers did, how the study was carried out and what they found. An analysis of it will include why the researcher chose to carry out the study in the way they did, the strengths and weaknesses in their approach and any gaps that might have been missed. Table 8.3 highlights some of the key differences between description and analysis.

Table 8.3: Some of the key differences between description and analysis

Description	Analysis
States what was done	Explains why things were done in particular ways
States what something is like	Explores why something is as it is
States how something is or was done	Considers a range of different ways something could, or should, have been done
Outlines a theory	Identifies strengths, weaknesses and gaps in a theory
Explains several theories	Compares and contrasts theories
Explains how an approach or approaches work	Considers why an approach or approaches work and why they might not in certain situations
Lists component parts	Considers different parts, one against the other

The table includes the word 'theory' and at this point you might want to look at some definitions of this that are included in Chapter 9. You will already know that in order to gain high marks for your literature review, and indeed for your dissertation as a whole, you will need to focus on analysis rather than description, so concentrating your efforts on the right-hand side of Table 8.3 will be important. But, advice from tutors can vary, which again can be confusing. Some tutors will say that some description is good because you need to introduce a topic to then be able to analyse it. Others (and this is my own view too) will say that words used on description are words lost from analysis. Here it is good to remember two things:

1. Describing something doesn't show that you have understood it and most importantly doesn't show how it relates to your research question. At best it shows that you can paraphrase from something published (for example, a book, an article) and at worst that you can copy and paste. In relation to plagiarism, please don't go there! Analysing something as set out in Table 8.3 enables you to show your knowledge and understanding.
2. Difficult as this is, tutors and supervisors vary in their advice. If you are in doubt about how much description to include (if any), remember to ask the tutor who will be marking your dissertation; and don't be surprised when you get different responses from different tutors.

Critical evaluation and synthesis are other important aspects of a strong literature review. In some respects, we have already covered the key aspects of critical evaluation, as this often involves comparing and contrasting approaches by focusing on their relative strengths and weaknesses. So, what do we mean by synthesis? Thomas (2017: 63) defines synthesis very clearly when he states that it involves bringing 'things together, relating one to another to form something new'. The final four words here highlight the important role of synthesis: to form something new. This is where your synthesis of the different arguments being made in literature in relation to your research question can, and should, highlight something new. So it is much more than a description of the published work of others, more than a presentation of the different arguments they make and is 'an intelligent appraisal of a range of sources that in some way extracts the key messages and accounts for them' (Thomas, 2017: 63) – all done in relation to your research question.

Finding those 'peachy' quotes

Direct quotes from literature form an important element of a strong literature review and selecting them is a skill. These form the guy ropes that support your Metaphorical Tent. I often use the word 'peachy' to describe a good quote; you will know one when you read it because it will make you think something like 'That's just great!' or 'That's just what I need!' This kind of quote has the following qualities:

- it is often quite short, just a few words or a single short sentence;
- it sums up an argument you are wanting to make;
- it highlights a key point that you are putting across;
- it provides a key reference in your work.

The first point is perhaps the most important one here; it is not too long. In general, my own advice is anything that is longer than two lines is too long; the shorter the better. Often students say to me things like 'But the writer says it so much better than I can' or 'The writer puts it so well and I feel like I'm not doing their work justice'. Often a short summary of their argument and a short quote to go with it will be much better than a lengthy quote left to stand on its own; remember to keep quotes short!

Some practical tips for carrying out a literature review

In Chapter 14 we consider a range of aspects of managing a desk-based project and at various points, it will probably be good to refer to this as your study progresses. Here we focus on some practical tips for the literature review process:

- take notes and keep them secure by saving them on your computer or by writing in a notebook rather than on loose sheets of paper;

- be sure to keep some kind of record of where you have found your key sources;
- consider compiling your reference list as you go along – a vital time-saver as your deadline looms;
- keep a record of page numbers for your direct quotes;
- consider learning a new approach to managing your references (for example, RefWorks) if you can pick it up quickly – if not, it's probably not worth it at this stage;
- be sure to use approaches that work for you.

Other questions that students often ask me in relation to a literature review include 'How do I know when to stop reading?' and 'How can I be sure that I haven't missed something vital?' As a general rule, you will know when to stop reading when you start to read things that are similar to what you have read already; this is known as literature saturation (Aveyard et al, 2016). You might find you get thoughts like 'This is similar to what x argues about this' or even 'It feels like I've read about this before'. In relation to missing something vital, if you have carried out a thorough search this shouldn't happen. Equally, no review can include everything and if you start your literature review with a short discussion of what you have selected and why, you will avoid this criticism.

What makes a strong reference list?

Many students ask me how many references should be in a good reference list for a dissertation. This is not an easy question to answer and will depend on the length of the dissertation. But, as a general guide, a strong reference list at undergraduate level will usually take up at least two to three pages. However, it is not only the number of references that matters, but the quality and range of them too.

Depending on the subject area and academic discipline, a strong reference list for a qualitative desk-based study will include the primary and secondary sources we discussed earlier. It will also include work that is current – as a general rule, things that have been published within the last five years. Any list that does not contain any literature like this could well be seen as dated and having a few items from this year or last year will make your list look right up to date. When referring to academic books, always be sure to use the latest edition, because again, this will make your list look current. However, it is good to be aware of two things: first, don't assume that the latest version contains exactly the same things as the previous one. It is a new edition for a reason and the parts you want to refer to may have changed as the author's ideas have developed over time. Second, it might be that the earlier edition contains more of what you need to refer to than the newer one; don't be afraid to make this point when writing up your literature review as this shows criticality and an eye for detail. You should then include both editions in your reference list.

A strong reference list also includes all seminal work in a given area. These are publications that have stood the test of time and are still relevant even though they were published some years ago. These will be specific to your topic area and your reference list probably won't look complete without them.

 Doing your reference list at the end is definitely a mistake to avoid. It will take much longer and, in my view, it is not the most interesting of tasks!

SUMMARY

In this chapter we have examined a number of aspects of the process of carrying out a literature review. It can be a large but very rewarding task and one that enables you to show knowledge and understanding of your topic. Be sure to seek advice from your library staff if you get stuck at any point. In the next chapter we move on to a discussion of desk-based methodologies in qualitative research.

Further reading

- Greetham (2021) offers a lot of practical detail on completing a literature review, including some of the common problems encountered by students and researchers.
- Eckstein (2018) provides a useful overview of the purpose of a literature review and includes helpful summaries of different types of literature to include and on finding high-quality sources.

9

Desk-based methodologies

In this chapter we will:

☐ discuss the term methodology in desk-based research – the groundsheet of the Metaphorical Tent;

☐ consider some of the possible theoretical underpinnings of qualitative research;

☐ explore some other key qualitative terms – epistemology, interpretivism, ontology and subjectivism – and contrast these with the terms used in quantitative research;

☐ consider issues of **validity, reliability** and **generalisability** in qualitative research;

☐ explain how to write a strong methodology section in a dissertation;

☐ bring this all together using a hierarchy of objectives.

In this chapter we move on to discuss a range of key concepts that come under the umbrella term methodology. The term methodology can be difficult to understand, and, in many ways, this is because it is abstract and intangible. Another key challenge is that clear definitions of a number of abstract terms in research can be surprisingly difficult to find and, as in other areas, academics don't always agree on their meaning. Many of my own students find this particular area difficult to grasp and indeed often say that the methodology section of their dissertation is the most difficult one to write; and they are not alone. In my own doctoral research, I found this whole area very difficult too and, in this chapter, at the risk of oversimplifying things, we will use a number of concrete examples in order to demystify this whole area to make it more understandable.

What do we mean by the term methodology?

We begin by looking at the term methodology and what it means. I have spent several hours searching for a clear definition of the word methodology, and I felt sure it must be out there somewhere. But the more I looked, the more variations I found. As Mackenzie and Knipe (2006: 5) suggest, 'a large number of texts provided no definition for the terms methodology or method, some texts use the terms interchangeably and others use them as having different meanings'. In the end it seems that methodology is a term that is not particularly clearly defined and is probably best understood as an umbrella term for a system for researching a particular area. A strong methodology underpins a strong piece of research, in the same way as a robust groundsheet provides a secure base for your Metaphorical Tent (see Figure 9.1).

Figure 9.1: The groundsheet

View from beneath

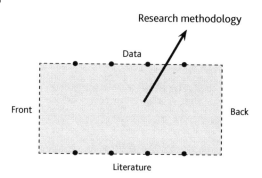

A strong methodology is guided by theory and provides a robust explanation of how we carried out a study and why we chose to do it in a particular way. Before we move on, we need to clarify what we mean by the term theory; again, this is something that academics and tutors do not always agree on and continue to debate. Thomas (2017) helpfully discusses the following five different meanings of the word theory.

1. A generalising or explanatory model – this is the kind of theory that seeks to draw together findings or observations in order to put forward general propositions of how things are perceived.
2. The 'thinking side' of practice – used in the applied social sciences (for example, social work, teaching, nursing) and often referred to as 'reflective practice' or 'practical theory' where explanations emerge from and are grounded in professional practice.
3. A developing body of explanation – here theory keeps knowledge in a particular area moving forward.
4. Scientific theory – explains ideas as a series of statements that can be tested, and also means that predictions can be made. In the social sciences this is becoming less common.
5. Grand theory – something that seeks to explain the nature of mankind and society broadly. Examples include Marx and Freud.

(Drawn from Thomas, 2017: 98)

In this book, the term theory is taken to mean an individual's (or two people's, or even a group of people's) explanation of a particular phenomenon, based on research, rather like Thomas' first point. This means it is much more than an idea, and it will have been researched and published in academic sources. My favourite quote in relation to theory comes from the seminal writer and theorist Kurt Lewin, who states 'There's nothing so practical as good theory' (Lewin, 1951: 169). To me this makes the whole idea of theory accessible and useful. As one of the founders of social and organisational psychology, Lewin was interested in theory that could be applied, particularly to organisational development. As a result, he developed the strategy of action research with its focus on bringing about change in organisations. This is theory that seeks explanations from practice (rather like Thomas' point 2), which in turn continues to develop a body of knowledge that moves forward (Thomas' point 3).

Theory can be seen to inform a research project in two ways: I call this theory from above and theory from below, where the research question is the focal point. This is shown in Figure 9.2.

Figure 9.2: Theory from above and theory from below

Theory from above (second side panel)

Literature review
(What is known and published in relation to your research question)

Research question

Research methods
(How you carried out research into your research question)

Theory from below (groundsheet)

Theory from above refers to the theory that you examine in a literature review or the second side panel of your Metaphorical Tent, what is already known and has been published in relation to your research question. We covered this in Chapter 8 in some depth. In this chapter we are focusing on theory from below, or the groundsheet; this is theory from the domain of research methods that offers explanations of how you carried out your research project and why. Both areas of theory need to be examined in some detail in a dissertation. In my experience, students can sometimes forget to include theory from below in their dissertation and this is probably because they covered it in an earlier research methods module, which might even have been studied in the previous academic year. Theory from below is about applying research methods theory to your own project, and this application gives you the opportunity to show you have understood it.

 You will probably need to go back to the literature you read in your research methods module when you start to write the methodology section of your dissertation, and to what you wrote in your research proposal.

Theory covered in research methods modules can vary too, as discussed in Chapter 1, and it is well worth checking what expectations are to make sure that you are meeting them. For example, if you demonstrate a clear understanding of the difference between qualitative and quantitative method, will that be enough, or will you also need to discuss things at the philosophical level of interpretivism and positivism? In some cases, you may need to go further and consider approaches to research such as constructivism, critical theory, ethnography, grounded theory, narrative, phenomenology and case study, if they apply to your own research. If this is the case, you will need to read some other sources. Biggam (2018) contains helpful sections on several of these and at the end of this chapter there are some more key texts you might wish to refer to in order to make sure you are meeting expectations.

 If you are unsure about any of this, do talk to your supervisor about what is usually expected, and in particular what will be needed in relation to your study.

Methodology then is a system that uses theory in order to explain the approach taken in a research project. How to write a strong methodology section will be discussed later in this chapter, but for now, we move on to the next 'ology' and that is epistemology.

Epistemology

Epistemology is the term used to describe knowledge, and in particular how we know what we know. It is defined as 'how we understand and research the world, and the warrants we use in validating our understanding' (Green, 2008, cited in Cohen et al, 2018: 32). There are different schools of thought within the philosophy of education and research regarding this, which can be summed up in the following two key paradigms (or groups of theories).

1. Positivism – from this philosophical viewpoint we research things through scientific enquiry in order to provide answers to questions or solutions to problems. Discussing the philosophical contribution of Auguste Comte, Hammersley (2013: 22) describes positivism as 'the modern scientific outlook that was in the process of replacing previously dominant supernatural ways of thinking about the world'. Positivism is all about the application of science and positivists tend to look for universal laws based on a hypothesis that is then tested. A very simple example here is that every time two atoms of hydrogen are put together with one atom of oxygen, you get water. It happens every time, can be done on any number of occasions with the same result and can be proved through the application of science. In the social sciences, positivism is generally the philosophical underpinning of quantitative research where a hypothesis is tested numerically to try and find a statistical correlation.

2. Interpretivism – from this philosophical viewpoint, the assertion is that in the social sciences things are often not as straightforward as in the example given in point 1; if the COVID–19 pandemic has taught us anything, it's that science isn't that straightforward either! However, in general, things are much less predictable when we study people, and different research participants often respond in different ways to the same issue. Discussing interpretivism, Hammersley (2013: 27) argues that 'people actively interpret or make sense of their environment and of themselves … shaped by the cultures in which they live'. As a result, there will be no single correct answer or solution, only multiple interpretations. The role of the interpretivist researcher is, as the term implies, to examine their non–numerical data (see Chapter 1) in order to interpret it and gain new insights. In the social sciences, this is generally the philosophical underpinning of qualitative research.

The focus in this book is on qualitative desk-based research underpinned by the philosophical viewpoint of interpretivism. However, showing a good grasp of both paradigms in the methodology section of your dissertation means you can demonstrate a broader and deeper level of understanding of your own philosophical position. We will come back to this later in the chapter.

Both theory from above and below (see Figure 9.2) form a theoretical framework for your research project and devising this framework gives you an opportunity to show your grasp of the epistemology of your study. Theory from above that you have critically evaluated in your literature review focuses on what has been published in relation to your research questions. Carrying out this review involves a process of synthesising the arguments being made in literature (see Chapter 8) and drawing them together to highlight something new. This often involves drawing the threads of different arguments being made together to reach new insights in relation to your research question. These insights are likely to emerge from your examination and interpretation of the range of arguments being made. By reviewing a number of primary sources (for example, academic journal articles and published research reports), you may also have become aware of the philosophical approach (positivist or interpretivist) taken by the researchers who have carried out the studies. All of this forms the theory from above that relates to your particular study. Theory from below is drawn from literature on research methods and offers explanations of how you carried out research into your own research question and why.

To form a theoretical framework for your study you will need to examine theory from above and theory from below. Here is what this includes for Emma and her study (see Figure 9.3).

Figure 9.3: Emma's theoretical framework

STOP

 Even though the focus here is on qualitative desk-based research, you might examine quantitative studies as part of your literature review, so having an understanding of positivism will be important too and ignoring it could be a problem.

Ontology

In your readings about methodology another 'ology' you will come across is ontology and this relates to the view of reality we adopt in our research. Philosophers have debated issues of reality over the centuries and you may have come across aspects of this in your everyday life, for example, the well-known question of 'If a tree falls in a forest and there is no one there to hear it, does it make a sound?' The general scientific conclusion on this is that sound is something experienced as an ear drum vibrates, so if nobody can observe or hear this, it is conjecture, and can't be proven. This highlights that reality can be a very difficult thing to define. O'Leary (2021: 6) explains ontology clearly and succinctly when she states that ontology is 'The study of what exists, and how things that exist are understood and categorized. Our personal ontology points to what we think is "real", what we think "exists".'

Returning to our discussion of epistemology, the links with ontology become apparent. If we adopt a single view of reality and believe there is, or will be, one answer or a clear solution or conclusion that will emerge from our study, we will adopt a positivist ontology. However, if we expect a range of answers or insights, we will adopt an interpretivist ontology. In this book, we focus on an interpretivist ontology because of its focus on qualitative desk-based research. This is in the light of an expectation of multiple insights gained from the analysis of data.

SAM

I've been busy reading some outlines of biographies of refugees. These tell stories of real struggles and contain some aspects that are similar. The most common ones are being separated from family, financial hardships and the challenges of building a new life. But also, some are very different, in particular how different people cope with similar challenges. I really don't think there will be a single outcome or conclusion from researching this area. I can see that it's all about how different people see things differently, so I think my study will have an interpretivist ontology – I need to get those words into my dissertation for sure!

Subjectivism and objectivism

Two other terms that you will probably come across in your reading of research methods literature are **objectivism** and subjectivism. Dictionary definitions of the word objective include phrases like 'based on fact' and 'not influenced by personal beliefs or feelings'. These chime closely with definitions of positivism and the application of science to research, often done in the social sciences by using quantitative methods. By contrast dictionary definitions of the term subjective use words like 'influenced or based on personal belief or feelings' and 'something based on opinion'. This basic dictionary definition can leave qualitative researchers feeling like the poor relation, with their research being seen as less valid and reliable and, as we shall see in the next section, this is far from the case. The word that is missing from this definition is interpretation and many social scientists appreciate that there is value in understanding how people understand experiences and issues differently.

In research the terms used are objectivist and subjectivist; these words are not included in a basic dictionary. The ending of 'ist' makes a big difference and highlights a particular approach being taken rather than any kind of claim being made. Rather than research being said to be objective or subjective it should be described as objectivist or subjectivist. Even in quantitative research it is arguable whether or not a study can be completely objective; we've probably heard the well-known phrase 'lies, damn lies and statistics' and all statistics are, after all, subject to interpretation. Given (2012a: 2) defines objectivism as 'the notion that an objective reality exists and can be increasingly known through the accumulation of more complete information'. This contrasts with her description of subjectivism as the 'interactions between researcher and subjects ... and the active interpretation of data' (Given, 2012b: 4). The words objectivist and subjectivist can be linked with other terms discussed already. A quantitative study can be described as having a positivist objectivist epistemology. By contrast, a qualitative desk-based study can be described as having an interpretivist subjectivist epistemology. These are great words for a methodology section in a dissertation. But remember, you need to show your understanding of them when you use them.

RAJESH

I've loved music for as long as I can remember. I've definitely got my own musical preferences and I know my friends and family have theirs too and they're very different. I feel like my understanding of how music helps people with issues of anxiety is growing all the time. I can hear stories of people in podcasts who find different genres of music helpful for very different reasons. I can see there is no 'one size fits all' in this area and that my approach can probably be described as an interpretivist subjectivist epistemology. I definitely need to use words like these when I'm writing the methodology section of my dissertation.

Validity, reliability and generalisability

We now move on to consider three more key research terms; the first two (validity and reliability) are easier to understand when considered together. In all research, issues of validity and reliability are important because they ensure that a study is robust, can stand up to some level of scrutiny and assessment, which in turn means that it is of good quality. Having a clear understanding of the terms themselves will help you to put forward a strong argument in your dissertation and posing the following two questions can help you in this regard:

- Validity – is the research measuring what it set out to measure, or exploring what it set out to explore?
- Reliability – if this research were carried out again in similar circumstances, would the results be approximately the same?

Heale and Twycross (2015: 66) give a simple but memorable example: 'an alarm clock rings at 7:00 each morning but is set for 6:30. It is reliable (it consistently rings at the same time each day) but is not valid (because it is not ringing at the time set).'

Validity and reliability are important for all research and are often easier to measure in a quantitative study. In a qualitative study both terms can present challenges because there is no agreement on how they should be measured, or even if they can be measured. Bearing in mind that taking an interpretivist approach to a study means an expectation of multiple interpretations and understandings, then other terms are needed in a desk-based qualitative study. Here, the concepts of validity and reliability are generally applied to the researcher rather than the study and different terms are often used. Qualitative research demonstrates that it is valid via the integrity of the researcher, how they explain their own position in the research (or positionality – see Chapter 3), how they have applied the method chosen and the accuracy involved in presenting the data. Many qualitative researchers prefer the term **trustworthiness** – in other words can the findings be trusted (Korstjens and Moser, 2018) – and use this instead of the term validity. A qualitative researcher needs to demonstrate that their work can be trusted by showing in detail that it was carried out systematically and with integrity. Reliability in qualitative research relates to the level of consistency employed in data analysis (Noble and Smith, 2015). In qualitative research there is no expectation that findings would be similar if the research were carried out again either by the same researcher or by someone else; interpretations will be different. But this does not make a researcher's interpretations any less worthwhile, as all qualitative research can offer new insights. Many qualitative researchers do not use the word reliability to describe their research as it is simply not about being able to replicate their research with other participants and in different situations and getting similar results. Instead, all qualitative researchers need to provide a detailed description of how they analysed their data to show they have used a thorough and considered approach and that their work can be relied upon to show meaningful insights.

We now move on to the third key term: generalisability. This is linked with the terms validity and reliability and refers to whether the findings from a research study could be applied in other similar circumstances or situations; in other words, could they be generalised to wider populations. As a term, generalisability is usually applied to quantitative research, like our example of water (H_2O), where this research can be shown to be the case more broadly. In qualitative research, the term generalisability is often replaced by the word **transferability** and means that the researcher provides sufficient evidence to show that the findings could be applied to other situations. This is often achieved by writing **thick descriptions** of how they carried out their research and how they analysed and interpreted their data to make it trustworthy (Korstjens and Moser, 2018). This is also a key element of data analysis (see Chapter 11). Any claims of generalisability and transferability in a qualitative desk-based study need to be stated tentatively, otherwise they would probably not stand up to scrutiny.

How to write a strong methodology section in a dissertation

As I mentioned earlier in this chapter, writing the methodology chapter was the most challenging aspect of writing my whole thesis. One day I attended a research group and decided to 'take the plunge' and share the difficulties I was having with the people there. The professor leading it gave me the following advice: 'Tell me the story of your research – what you did and why.' At the time this was revelatory to me and instantly made the task of writing my methodology chapter seem doable. This turned out to be some of the most helpful advice I ever had while studying at doctoral level. I went away from the group meeting and wrote the first draft of my methodology chapter in record time!

Since then, I have often used this phrase and have added some words of my own. 'Tell me the story of your research – what you did and why, and what you didn't do and why not.' This is because when writing my own methodology chapter, I quickly realised it was very descriptive. By writing about what I didn't do and the reasons for this as well, the chapter became a critical evaluation of my study rather than a description. Irrespective of the level of study, this is what I believe is needed for a strong methodology section.

The topic of the next chapter is data analysis and my own students often ask me where they should write about how they analysed their data. My own view is that this is best done towards the end of the methodology section as it completes the picture of the whole research process. However, some supervisors prefer it to be included within the data analysis section.

 If you're not sure about where to write about how you analysed your data, it is always best to check with your supervisor.

Understanding methodology using a hierarchy of objectives

Around the same time, my own supervisor said to me 'Think of your methodology section as a hierarchy of objectives, where you can track your study from top to bottom, or from bottom to top, starting at any point.' This proved to be another invaluable piece of advice. A strong methodology section is best written as a critical evaluation of your study and this can be done by using a hierarchy of objectives. A hierarchy of objectives is a visual and practical tool that enables the analysis of a project in a step–by–step, or level–by–level, way. Figure 9.4 shows this.

If we take the example of a qualitative study on the right–hand side of the diagram, this uses an interpretivist approach. The epistemology and ontology are subjectivist because it is accepted that there will be multiple realities as distinct from one single reality or solution. A qualitative method is used to gather non–numerical data. By contrast on the left–hand side a quantitative desk–based study uses a positivist approach. The epistemology and ontology are objectivist in the expectation of finding a single reality by testing a hypothesis. A quantitative method is used to gather numerical data.

Writing a methodology section can be done very effectively by using this hierarchy, either from top to bottom or from bottom to top. In my experience, many students find it easier to do this from bottom to top, at least initially (see Figure 9.5). So, starting at the bottom, a qualitative desk–based study involves examining non–numerical data (for example, videos, podcasts, journal entries or other documents) from a subjectivist ontology that assumes multiple realities. The epistemology assumes there is no single view or solution, but that knowledge is built through interpretation (or interpretivism). By contrast, a quantitative desk–based study involves examining numerical data (for example, surveys and statistical studies) from an objectivist ontology that assumes a single reality. The epistemology assumes there is a single view or solution, and that knowledge is built through scientific application or positivism.

Writing a strong methodology section involves engaging with both sides of the hierarchy of objectives. This means you avoid work that is too descriptive, enabling you to put forward a stronger justification of how you carried out your study and why. In addition, you will be able to show a greater breadth of understanding of research methods, which should all help you to gain a higher mark.

Supervisors do not all agree on whether you should write about what you didn't do and why not. Some say it is sufficient to focus on what you did and why. So, be sure to check this out with them, as they will be marking your work.

Figure 9.4: A hierarchy of objectives in empirical research

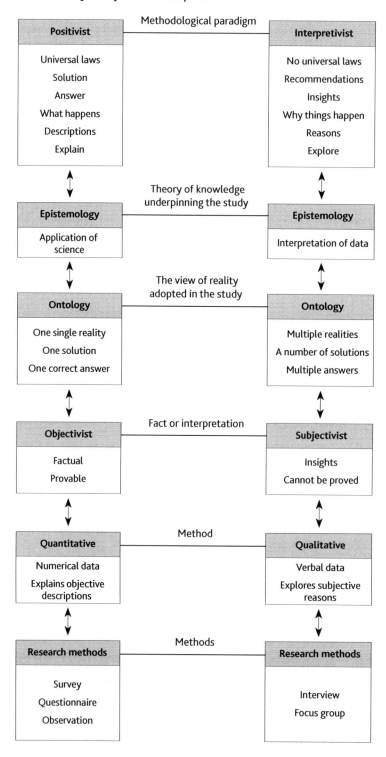

Figure 9.5: Hierarchy of objectives in qualitative desk-based research

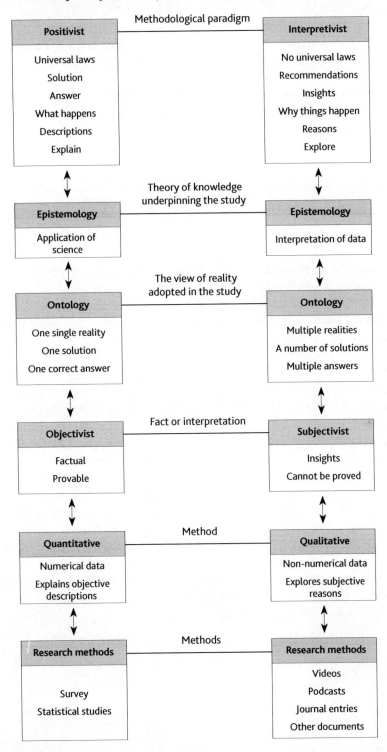

SUMMARY

In this chapter we have continued to erect the Metaphorical Tent, focusing on the groundsheet, which represents methodology in a qualitative desk-based study. Terminology in this area can be challenging and if you don't understand something straight away, don't be afraid to reread some key texts and to ask your tutor or supervisor to explain things again. This should ultimately enable you to write a strong and critically reflective methodology section in your dissertation. In the next chapter we move on to examine the whole area of research ethics.

Further reading

- Bryman (2016) offers an excellent chapter (Chapter 2) explaining a range of challenging methodological terms in an accessible way.

In addition, here is a list of extra texts you might want or need to read that relate to more specific qualitative approaches.

- Bronner (2017) is a relatively short book that gives an excellent introduction to critical theory, robustly outlining its history and philosophical development.
- Hammersley and Atkinson (2019) has a thorough explanation of ethnography and Chapter 1, 'What is ethnography', gives a very clear explanation of this approach.
- Squire et al (2014) present a practical introduction to narrative research designed for beginners who want to build their knowledge and skills in this approach.
- Tarozzi (2020) contains very clear explanations of grounded theory and Part I of the book gives a thorough introduction to the origins of grounded theory, including its historical context and an evaluation of the approach.
- Tatano Beck (2021) is a detailed and accessible book on different theoretical approaches to phenomenology. It also contains an engaging introduction to this whole area that is applicable to a number of different academic disciplines.
- Twomey Fosnot (2005) contains an excellent chapter on the philosophy of constructivism (Chapter 1) written by von Glasersfeld.
- Yin (2018) is the 'go-to' book on case study research for many researchers. It takes a clear and thorough approach, including reasons why people choose this approach and why they don't.

10

Ethics

In this chapter we will:

☐ discuss the term ethics in desk-based research – the footprint groundsheet of the Metaphorical Tent;

☐ examine some key ethical principles and frameworks in research;

☐ explore the importance of anonymity;

☐ consider confidentiality, the General Data Protection Regulation (GDPR) and issues of copyright;

☐ examine how to get informed consent;

☐ consider the ethics of self-care in research.

The focus of this chapter is on the ethics of qualitative desk-based research and will include an examination of a range of important terms that you need to pay attention to throughout your research project. A consideration of relevant ethical issues was part of the process of writing your research proposal, which may have been considered by an ethics committee or panel within your university (see Chapter 4). It is important to pay attention to ethical issues at every step as your project unfolds, including how and where you store your data. These issues also need to be borne in mind and reflected on when writing your dissertation. All research must be carried out in line with some key ethical principles and, while it might be tempting to think that data drawn from the internet lies outside many of the boundaries of ethics because it is already in the public domain, this is rarely the case. In this chapter, we explore how these ethical principles apply to qualitative desk-based research in particular.

Ethics form the footprint groundsheet of your Metaphorical Tent (see Figure 10.1). A footprint groundsheet is a piece of waterproof tarpaulin cut to the exact size of the bottom of your tent and it serves a number of functions. As well as giving an extra layer of waterproofing and insulation, it keeps your tent clean and dry, which makes it last longer; securing it in the ground first means you then know exactly where to pitch your tent. In the same way, a thorough consideration of relevant ethical issues goes a long way in ensuring that your

Figure 10.1: The footprint groundsheet

View from beneath

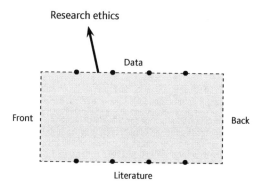

research project is protected and will be well received in the academic community, including those who will mark your dissertation.

Ethics in research

Ethics is a term that is used relatively frequently in everyday language and we might hear a phrase like 'that's not very ethical is it?', or something similar, from time to time. Although we might know in general terms what this means, it is useful to look at a definition of ethics here, particularly in the context of research. Ethics is often described as a branch of philosophy that deals with morals, in other words, how people are meant to behave. The discipline of ethics seeks to describe broad terms like good and evil, right and wrong, virtue and vice, justice and injustice. The territory of ethics is complex and contested; it also changes over time as new knowledge and practices continually emerge, and societies progress. We only have to look at the growth of social media and its effects on people's lives to see evidence of rapid change in ways of thinking in this area. Ethics applies to most areas of everyday life and every parent knows that there is a lot of groundwork involved in helping children from a very early age to understand the difference between right and wrong. As children grow into adolescence, the complexities become more evident as young people start to consider the choices they have in areas of life that are often blurred and not clear–cut.

Research ethics provide a set of beliefs and subsequent behaviours that guide us through the whole of the research process, from putting together a proposal to doing the final writing up. In simple terms, it is all about 'doing things right', and throughout, a reflexive researcher (see Chapter 3) will be in tune with their emotions as these may well highlight potential ethical issues. Boyd and Fales (1983) use the term 'inner discomfort' to describe the feelings we might experience during the reflective process more broadly; we can also experience these feelings at times during the reflective research process. This inner discomfort might prompt thoughts like 'this doesn't feel quite right' or 'I wonder if I should be doing this', which should act as a guide to our behaviour. It is well worth recording these instances in your research journal as they happen, as this will give you a reminder of things you will want to reflect on at a later date, either as you write the methodology section or as part of the reflective evaluation of your study.

 Writing in your research journal is a great way of capturing your thoughts as they occur and really helps your developing understanding.

In relation to ethics, Largan and Morris (2019: 100) identify the following six key duties and responsibilities of researchers.

1. Researcher integrity – the term integrity means being honest and having strong moral principles that are applied consistently. Researcher integrity includes such things as making your own position clear (the issue of positionality as discussed in Chapter 9) to address any potential issues of bias and being honest and transparent with any data you gather. This includes not trying to 'shoehorn' your data into what you expected to find, but then didn't.
2. Respecting intellectual property rights – these are rights given to individuals, groups and companies to protect their original ideas and include issues of copyright. Respecting these rights means being mindful of the duty not to steal someone else's work and always to refer to the originators in an appropriate way. By now you will be used to doing this in the way you reference the things you have read and, as a result, understand the dangers associated with plagiarism.
3. Following codes of conduct – ethical researchers need codes of conduct to guide them. All universities have published ethical codes and you will want to refer to your own university's code during your study. There may be other codes you will want to refer to as well, such as the code of the British Educational Research Association (BERA) and perhaps those from relevant professional associations.
4. Morals (personal beliefs) – this is a tricky area and is one that you might well need to address at various points through critical reflection. People think differently about similar things and what one person finds comfortable, another may not. This takes us into the whole arena of personal judgement; again, it is good to be aware of any inner discomfort you might be feeling and allow this to guide your responses and actions.
5. Respect – this is a word we use a lot in everyday language and again can mean different things to different people. It can be summed up as 'treat others as you would like to be treated'. In other words, be aware of people's feelings, wishes, rights and interests and act accordingly.
6. Compliance with legal frameworks – in research this particularly applies to issues of confidentiality, anonymity and data protection.

Being an ethical researcher involves fulfilling each of these six key duties.

If you are unsure at any point about whether or not you are carrying out your research ethically, do be sure to talk to your supervisor. This discussion will help you to 'unpick' the situation and find a way forward.

Some key ethical principles for research

Ethics in research first came to the fore in the aftermath of the Second World War, a time when serious atrocities carried out previously in a number of countries became apparent. Examples include the Tuskegee Syphilis Study of 1932–1972 in Alabama, and the Monster Study carried out in Iowa in 1939; both of these (and others) are well documented online and in research methods texts. Today both studies would be seen as completely unacceptable because of the lasting damage they did to the innocent and unknowing participants, some of whom were children. Quite rightly such studies are now seen as dehumanising.

Another big influence on the world of ethics has been that of the medical profession. This isn't surprising when you consider the challenging decisions that need to be made every day regarding such things as who gets surgery, treatment or a vaccine first and so on, when usually it isn't possible, or even desirable, for everyone to get everything. Beauchamp and Childress (2019) first published their seminal work on biomedical ethics in 1979 where they outlined four key principles to ethical practice. These are:

1. **Autonomy** – people have the right to make their own decisions and this should always be respected. Patients need to be able to make these decisions in an informed way without any undue influence from the professional concerned and with any possible risks involved made clear.
2. **Non–maleficence** – do no harm. All action taken needs to be made with this in mind and will inevitably be done within the confines of knowledge and understanding at the time.
3. *Beneficence* – do good. This is the opposite of non–maleficence and can sometimes be called into question in relation to research findings. In particular, findings always need to be written with integrity, even when they might be unpalatable.
4. *Justice* – the greatest good for the greatest number. This is a reminder of utilitarian ethics and will not always apply to research.

These principles have now been applied to many different professional fields and while all four can be applied to research, the first two in particular point to some important ethical issues.

All research findings need to be reported with integrity, even if they do not appear positive. In addition, if it turns out that your research does not reveal what you expected, this may well be a strength not a weakness. It will mean that your study is showing something different (for example, a new insight), which is good, and it will give you lots to reflect on in the evaluation of your study.

 Always act with researcher integrity.

Four key ethical principles in desk-based research

In general terms there are four key ethical principles that need some careful consideration at every step of the research process; these are informed consent, maintaining confidentiality, anonymity and researcher integrity. These all link with the concepts of autonomy and non-maleficence (Beauchamp and Childress, 2019) and are shown in Figure 10.2.

Figure 10.2: Four key ethical principles in desk-based research

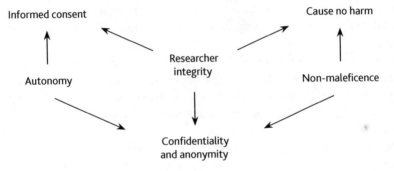

Researcher integrity lies at the centre because it influences everything researchers do. It means that we need to gain informed consent from participants, maintain their anonymity and keep their data confidential. This means that as far as possible, our research does no harm.

We will now consider the principles of gaining informed consent and maintaining anonymity and confidentiality in relation to desk-based research.

Informed consent

This principle means that all research participants have the right to make their own decisions about whether or not to take part in a study. They have a right to autonomy and to make this decision for themselves, without being persuaded or coerced in any way. They also have the right to withdraw their consent at any time and, thereby, to withdraw from the study. Their decisions should always be respected, even when, for example, their withdrawal might be disappointing for us as researchers. Informed consent means that researchers have a duty to let participants know from the beginning 'what they are in for' by sharing details of the project in a clear and understandable way, so they can make an informed decision. This is usually best done through an information sheet that is designed either as part of a signed consent form or as an additional sheet. This information sheet should outline what the study is about, what it is for (for example, for a dissertation) and who will read it.

In some areas of desk-based research, the issue of informed consent is relatively clear-cut, depending on your data resource. For instance, if you plan to analyse published minutes of formal meetings (for example, from educational institutions, large companies, local authorities or government departments) you may feel that gaining consent is not necessary because they have already been prepared for the public domain. This means they have been written by professionally trained minute-takers and scrutinised by managers for such things as keeping relevant details confidential, before being made public. They are very unlikely to contain any personal details and gaining consent to use them is probably unnecessary. The same might apply to using biographies published by reputable publishing houses. These too will have gone through a number of editorial processes, where the author will have made clear decisions about aspects of their story that they are happy to share with the public in a lasting way. In relation to my own publications I have often had the thought 'once it's out there, it's out there' and authors are rightly very mindful of their reputations. Although I have never written a biography, I imagine it involves making some careful decisions about what to leave out as well as what to include. Biographies that are self-published might be different though, as authors will not have had the opportunity to work with an editor or a team of reviewers. In these circumstances gaining consent might be important and, in general, many authors can be contacted directly either through a publishing (including a self-publishing) house's website or via professional networking sites (such as LinkedIn).

TIP **Most universities have templates for students to use when they need to request informed consent. These have been carefully worded to meet ethical codes, so do use them. They will also save you lots of time, which is always good!**

However, gaining informed consent for other sources that contain more personal data can be much more tricky. On one level it could be argued that if someone has made their details very public (for example, on the internet via a blog), they have already given their consent for others to see it. But in most cases, it is very unlikely that the material given was intended for research purposes. This means that the material will be subject to an analysis in relation to research questions and you could argue that this means treating that material very differently from anything they originally imagined when they first wrote it. In situations like this, an ethical approach is to try and gain informed consent wherever possible, by making every effort to contact the person concerned. But again, this can be problematic; people posting online sometimes use a pseudonym, which can make contact difficult and even impossible. Those who post via a platform can be contacted via messaging on that platform, but others who have their own individual blogs may be much more difficult to trace. It is clear that it won't always be possible to gain informed consent, especially when it comes to data drawn from the internet. But the generally accepted principle here is that you need to show that you have tried in whatever way you can. Keeping a record in your research journal of what you have done will be very useful as you will need to go back to this when writing about ethics in the methodology section of your dissertation.

SAM

I've found this great book that contains 19 biographies of refugees and now I'm thinking through the ethics of my study. The biographies tell some great stories and have been written by an academic. The book was published by a large professional publisher and lots of people have read it. I've also found a book written by the same author that takes a much more academic approach to the subject of the experiences of refugees. So, I don't feel there is a need to seek informed consent to use the stories but, to be on the safe side, I'll email my supervisor about it.

My supervisor has said that I could make contact with the author via the publisher's website and because the books are written by an academic, it should be quite easy to contact them directly. My supervisor also said they're confident that because the author is an academic, they are likely to give me permission for me to use their work in my research project. This is great and my supervisor has helped me to write an email to send to them. I'm keeping a copy of the email to include as an appendix to my dissertation and the notes on our discussion in case they are needed later on in my research journal.

Confidentiality and anonymity

These two concepts are closely linked and are best considered together rather than separately; they relate closely to issues of privacy and data protection. At the time of writing, data protection in the UK is still covered by the GDPR and is enshrined in law. GDPR is a legal framework that sets guidelines for the collection and processing of personal information from people who live in the European Union (EU). Your university's code of ethics for research will pay due attention to this and to anything that might replace it. All research participants rightly expect their data to be kept confidential and not to be shared with anyone else; this includes other participants, fellow students and supervisors. Ordinarily this means limiting access to the data to the researcher, only using the data for the purposes of the study, keeping it secure (for example, password-protected) and private (out of the sight of other people). A final measure is to destroy all the data collected when the study is complete. In empirical research participants are quite likely to disclose personal things about themselves and this is all done in an atmosphere of trust. This is where issues of anonymity come to the fore in order to ensure that no participant can be identified. This means giving each participant an appropriate pseudonym, one that represents their cultural and/ or ethnic heritage. In addition, organisations and locations should be made anonymous too. Ethical research respects human dignity and privacy; it is good to remember that research participants give their information freely and voluntarily and we should always handle it with respect and care.

 Maintaining the anonymity of research participants goes a long way in making sure that no harm is caused to them (non-maleficence). Always be vigilant about adapting details and not using anything that can identify individuals and organisations.

It is all too easy to assume that because someone has already made aspects of their life very public (for example, on the internet via a website), they have placed themselves outside the realm of confidentiality and anonymity; but this is not really the case. Many of the points made in this chapter also apply to desk-based research where issues of confidentiality and anonymity are no less important. However, ensuring anonymity can be complex and we need to be careful not to disclose the identity of someone, even though they have shared their data publicly. It is easy to do this inadvertently, for example by using the address of a particular website; this may contain access to an email address, which could identify a particular individual. Issues of privacy are no less important, and a high level of care also needs to be taken with online data to ensure that nothing is being disclosed that is of a sensitive or personal nature.

 Participants in desk-based research often do not have the right to withdraw from a study; this means we need to be even more careful in securing their anonymity and in the care we take of their data.

EMMA

I've now found a number of TV documentaries exploring issues of reoffending among young people. These are going to give me some rich data for analysis in relation to a number of key factors that influence the reoffending process. I know the young people in the documentaries will have given their consent to appear in the programmes, but I feel uncomfortable with drawing attention to them. This could disclose their identities further through my research. So, I think I need to keep the locations and names of the young offenders' institutions anonymous. It feels like I have to disclose details of the documentaries themselves because if I don't, this could make my data appear too weak for a robust academic study.

Self-care in research

Finally, we move on to consider issues of self-care in research. Causing no harm to research participants has been discussed and documented for many years, but a consideration of the harm that might be caused to researchers in the process of carrying out their studies has been much slower to emerge. Self-care in research is still a relatively new issue that remains largely undiscussed. Etherington (2004) mentions it in passing, but much more recently Kumar and Cavallaro (2018) address this issue more closely by including aspects of researcher stories that show some of the challenges they faced when gathering data on sensitive topics. These challenges can come to the surface whether or not researchers have had similar experiences to those they are researching. However, it seems fair to say that if you know you have experienced particularly challenging situations and circumstances, it is good to be especially aware of any feelings that your research might prompt in you. Often, we choose a particular topic because of the experiences we have had, or, like Sam, because of the experiences of those who are close to us. So, an important aspect of researcher reflexivity (see Chapter 3) is to be in tune with our feelings.

All of this applies to desk-based research too and we mustn't forget that written stories, documentaries or whatever kind of data we choose to use can prompt memories and feelings from the past, with the feelings often coming first as a preliminary warning (Berne, 1961). Just because we are not speaking to people directly does not mean that difficult memories will not come to the surface. In order to protect ourselves, we need to be aware of who we will go to for support at such times; this could be family and friends, a supervisor or student support and wellbeing.

RAJESH

I'm using a number of podcasts to explore how music has helped particular people to deal with issues of anxiety. I'm realising that these contain some personal and sensitive data. The people themselves are obviously happy to share their personal stories, but I can see that my analysis of them could lead to some insights that might not present them in a wholly positive way. I really think I need to give them anonymity so I'm going to think of some appropriate pseudonyms. I think I need to be careful when referring to other things too, such as their well-known recordings that would make them really easy to identify. It's interesting too that I'm being reminded of my own experiences as I listen to some of the podcasts. These final steps to gaining my degree mean that it's a challenging time, so I've decided to contact the person I know in student wellbeing for a chat. I'm going to speak to my supervisor about how I'm feeling too, and I've asked my close friends to keep an eye out for the things they all know can happen to me when I get anxious.

SUMMARY

We have considered a number of ethical issues in this chapter and many are linked with researcher integrity. As your study progresses, it is good to keep an eye on any ethical issues that might emerge and to remember to look out for yourself too. This is all part of making sure you succeed and complete a high-quality dissertation. In the next chapter we move on to data analysis.

Further reading

- Oliver (2010) is an accessible introduction to the role of ethics in research and is written specifically for students.
- Wiles (2013) gives a thorough account of the history of ethics and considers a wide range of issues relevant to qualitative research.

11

Data analysis and techniques

In this chapter we will:

☐ consider a number of ways to analyse data in qualitative desk-based research;

☐ revisit the canvas on the left-hand side of your Metaphorical Tent and the Research Triangle;

☐ discuss **inductive reasoning** and **deductive reasoning**;

☐ examine the most common techniques used when analysing qualitative data;

☐ examine some criteria to help you select the most appropriate analytical technique for your study;

☐ examine the importance of referring back to literature that you included in your review.

Having chosen a topic that you are really interested in, you are likely to gather data that you find really interesting too. If you find your data particularly compelling in some way, it is easy to think that what it says is in some way obvious and that it speaks for itself – the temptation then is to simply describe it in your dissertation. This is a common mistake; in practice, the next step is to move from data description to data analysis by undertaking a detailed and in–depth examination using your skills of criticality (see Chapter 3). In this chapter we consider the most common techniques of data analysis used in qualitative research. Using one, or a combination, of these can be very helpful in ensuring that your analysis is robust and leads to deep insights, one of the particular strengths of all types of qualitative research. Data analysis is the second part of the left–hand side of your Metaphorical Tent (see Figure 11.1).

There are a variety of views among academics about when data analysis starts in qualitative research. In empirical research, many argue that it starts after the interviews with the participants (the most common of qualitative research methods) and during the process of transcribing them. For example, Kowal and O'Connell (2014) describe transcribing interviews as a crucial step of data analysis, and Stuckey (2014) is more specific when she describes it as the first step of that

Figure 11.1: Data analysis and the Metaphorical Tent

View from the back

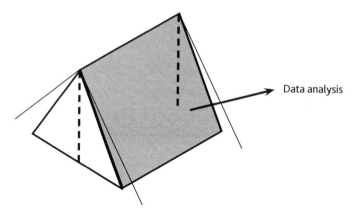

Data analysis

process. However, others argue that in qualitative research data analysis starts as soon as we start to collect data (Largan and Morris, 2019). Bearing in mind that qualitative research is interpretivist, as soon as we begin to look at particular data sources, we can't help but start a process of analysis and interpretation. We select particular resources because of what we think they can tell us and the insights they might give in relation to our research question, and we reject others for similar reasons. So the view taken here is that data analysis starts as soon as we start to collect data.

This became particularly clear to me at the very beginning of my own empirical qualitative research for my doctoral studies. I had arranged to carry out a small number of interviews with college students about how they were making their university choices with a view to trying to get some new insights in relation to a theoretical perspective that hadn't been explored before in my professional field. I hoped this might lead to some new thick descriptions of career development more broadly. The very first participant in the study (Tommy – a pseudonym I gave him to protect his anonymity) used a metaphor when discussing how he saw the process of choosing universities with the support of his careers adviser. I can still hear him speaking now and the clear description his actual words gave of the possible application of the particular theoretical approach to careers practice. This was a landmark point at the very beginning of data collection; I started the process of data analysis there and then. By sharing this I am not implying that this always happens, or even that it happens very often, but that we need to be ready for it, if and when it does. From this point on I understood that for me data analysis begins as soon as we start collecting data. Whether this is in an interview (as happened to me), or while watching a documentary, reading personal journals or documents online, the same principle applies.

Whenever you find data that really stands out to you in relation to your research question, be sure to write about it in your research journal. This will help you to process what you have found and take you a step further in analysing your data.

Inductive and deductive reasoning

When considering the whole area of data analysis in research, two other key terms come to the fore, **inductive reasoning** and **deductive reasoning**. We have already established that data analysis is much more than data description and here we need to consider the term critical reasoning as a foundation for understanding what inductive and deductive reasoning are in research. In Chapter 3 we discussed critical thinking as a key skill for researchers. This involves questioning everything, taking nothing for granted and not accepting anything at face value. Critical reasoning goes one or even several steps further. As we question, we analyse and interpret information in order to reach some conclusions based on the evidence we are presented with. Overall, this is a logical cognitive process and is a significant way in which we build our knowledge, not forgetting though that we have emotional reactions to evidence too.

Adding the words inductive and deductive serves to describe particular types of reasoning used in research (see Figure 11.2). Understanding these terms will help you to continue to add to the 'theory from below' that is guiding your research project (see Chapter 9). Here are definitions and explanations of these terms:

- Inductive reasoning – this is often described as moving from small to big. This involves making broad generalisations from a number of observations. At

Figure 11.2: Inductive and deductive reasoning

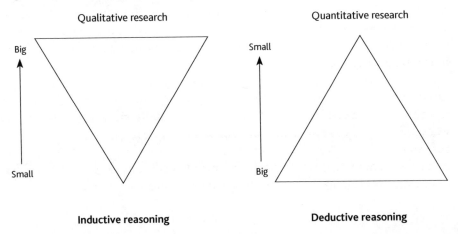

the risk of oversimplifying things, this is more commonly used in qualitative research. Remember though the points made in Chapter 9 in relation to issues of generalisability and the problems in applying the findings from a small research study to other similar circumstances or situations. We always need to be cautious when doing this and the language we use needs to be tentative.

- Deductive reasoning – this is often described as moving from big to small. This involves starting with a hypothesis or a general explanation and then testing it out in a particular situation or context. Overall, this is more commonly used in quantitative research.

Four common techniques of data analysis in qualitative research

There are a number of different techniques that can be used when analysing qualitative data and here we will look briefly at four of the most common ones. These all help you to engage in inductive reasoning to gain new insights in relation to your research question via a thorough examination, leading to your own interpretation. Largan and Morris (2019: 235) helpfully describe this as turning '"raw" data into something meaningful'. The most common techniques for analysing qualitative data are:

- thematic analysis (by far the most common)
- **content analysis**
- **narrative analysis**
- **discourse analysis**

In some studies, these are used on their own while in others they are combined. In particular, thematic analysis is often combined with others because this can lead to a more in-depth examination of the data concerned.

At the beginning of the data analysis process you will need to immerse yourself in your data. Empirical researchers do this when they transcribe their participant interviews; in desk-based research this can include things like reading texts, watching videos or listening to podcasts multiple times and carefully taking detailed notes. These notes will be used later when coding the data, a very common step in the data analysis process.

 Some videos (for example, those on YouTube) give you the option of viewing a transcript. Reading this with the video playing and on its own will probably make analysis easier. Saving the transcript can be very useful when coding the data later.

Thematic analysis

This is by far the most common technique used when analysing qualitative data, so much so that Tight (2019: 158) describes it as 'the most obvious strategy to take'. Thematic analysis happens as you immerse yourself in your data and involves a close examination of it to identify words, themes and phrases that recur, or that seem particularly significant in relation to your research question. You can then group these into categories using headings. There might well be several steps involved here as you revisit your data to delve deeply into it. As you progress, you may well want to link some of your headings together as you find connections between them.

It is good to be practical; data analysis doesn't need to be fancy and there is much to be said for keeping things simple. For example, you can take a photograph of your handwritten notes, or copy and paste your typed notes, print them, cut them up and stick them on a big sheet of paper under headings. This can be very helpful if you like to see things visually and it makes it easier to see connections between aspects of the data. Equally, you can use simple techniques like highlighting words and phrases in different colours using a word processor to make themes clear. Do whatever you find easiest and most helpful to you.

Content analysis

This involves examining data to discover how many times things are said or written and while it is most often associated with quantitative research, qualitative researchers use it too. I know I have described it to my students as 'a quantitative approach to analysing qualitative data', which doesn't sound particularly helpful or positive! But there is no doubt that the more times a word or phrase is used, the more significant it might well be, so analysing data in this way cannot be ignored. The process of content analysis is similar to that of thematic analysis discussed earlier and can be done in similar ways. A useful technique is using a word cloud which shows words being used most frequently as large text with other words being used decreasing proportionately in size. You could include this as an appendix to your dissertation as a visual aid for the reader, to show how you analysed your data.

RAJESH'S DATA ANALYSIS: CONTENT ANALYSIS WITH THEMATIC ANALYSIS

Having done some more research, I'm beginning to see the difference between the way listening to music can alleviate stress in general and music as a particular form of therapy for people with anxiety issues. I've found material online about a number of prominent people who have found music helpful when experiencing anxiety and stress. I'm particularly interested that one of my favourite comedians suffers with mental health issues and I never would have imagined that. He describes how music helped him during some very dark times in his life. He also speaks of how counselling helped him. I've found written material and a recording of a radio interview that he did, and I think together these could be one data resource for this study. I've also found a series of podcasts from the British Association for Music Therapy which include discussions on a range of mental health issues. I'm going to focus on one that relates to broader issues of anxiety given by a music therapist who is working in a community setting.

I've started the process of data analysis by reading through the online written material carefully and noting words that are used several times; these include stress is normal, failing to take time off, not speaking about mental health, a base level of anxiety and suicidal thoughts. I'm going through a similar process when listening to the podcast by the music therapist and the words most commonly used here include skills, psychodynamics and community. The words that really stand out to me are emotions, health and anxiety, which are used less frequently and I'm interested in the speaker's concept of 'trickle down' as a way of describing how music in the community can lead to more music in the home and its therapeutic benefits. I'm not going to include the word skills as this refers to training for music therapists, which doesn't really relate to my research question. I can definitely see three key themes: therapeutic interventions, community settings and mental health issues, and I'm giving each of them a code (TI, CS and MHI, so they're easy to remember). Now I need to use the codes to mark the relevant words from both the written material and the podcast. The great thing is the podcasts have a transcript with them, so this makes everything a fair bit quicker than it would be otherwise.

Now I'm thinking about my literature review as well. I thought it was complete, but I can see I've definitely got bits missing. I need to go back and read more about psychodynamics, which they seem to talk a lot about. I can see now what my supervisor meant when they said I need to think about the theory underpinning my study and I think I've probably found it! Or at least one piece of theory that's very relevant. I'm going back to my research questions too and will amend them to say something about music therapy.

Even if something is said or written only once but you feel it is particularly significant for your study, do take note of it. In my research, Tommy was the only student to describe his experience in the way he did, but I knew it was very significant for my study.

Narrative analysis

The focus of narrative research is on the story being told. Stories have a beginning, middle and end and there is a sense of chronology to them, experiences and events that happen in an order rather than in a random way. The story as a whole is important, as well as the different aspects of it. Using narrative analysis in desk-based qualitative research means seeking an in-depth understanding of the stories people are telling, whether these are in written, audio or some kind of visual form. Part of this is trying to get a view of how they see the world. This will involve examining the story itself and how it is being told. It may well also be important to consider who the story is written for and whether or not there is a stated purpose for it. Narrative analysis can involve the examination of a single text, like a biography or autobiography, or more than one. In other instances, you might use a number of personal journals or sequential blog entries, for example. Here your analysis will also involve constructing the story being told, as it may well be very fragmented.

SAM'S RESEARCH: NARRATIVE ANALYSIS WITH THEMATIC ANALYSIS

I've decided to use two data resources on the experiences of refugees and am starting to read them. It really feels like the process of analysis has begun and so I'm going to make some detailed notes while reading. Both of the books have been written by Viet Thanh Nguyen, a child refugee during the Vietnam war, now living in the US and an academic at the University of Southern California. I got a lovely email from him saying I could use his work in my project and he's even said he'd like to read it after I've submitted it, if I'd be happy with that. Let's see what mark I get first!

The first book, called *The Displaced*, begins with him telling the story of his own experiences, followed by the stories of 19 other refugees from different parts of the world. These stories have been edited by him. The other book is called *Nothing Ever Dies* and is a more theoretical examination of the lives of refugees and their experiences of war as the author reflects on his own life. Both books focus on the stories of refugees, so I think narrative analysis could be a good approach to use for my data analysis.

The stories the refugees tell are really compelling. It's taking me ages to read them and it feels like I'm trying to take in every word. Even though the refugees are from many different parts of the world, there are so many striking similarities with the words used by my mum in her stories over the years. Like Mum's story, these are also stories of war and conflict. In Nguyen's story, I can't believe the words he uses when describing the moment of escape as a 'life and death decision' his mum had to make on her own. This is exactly what my mum has said so many times.

I can see that the stories have a beginning (escape from violent conflict), middle (refugee camp) and end, or rather continuation of challenges and conflict (racism, injustice, search for identity). I'm now using these words when making notes, and it's turned into a template that I can use while making notes on the other stories. This is making aspects of the stories much clearer. I can see four themes emerging – fleeing from conflict, loss, trauma and memory. I'm using four different coloured highlighter pens to make the themes clear and I can already see some links between them, especially between trauma and memory. Our brains are very clever, and they remember so much. But what about the things we'd really like to forget?

The second text that Sam analyses is more theoretical and contains a lot of helpful links with academic literature. Reading this reminds Sam of the Research Triangle and the need to go back to the literature review and to read a few more key texts, particularly in relation to memory, something Sam hasn't really identified so far.

 During the process of data analysis, you may well find that you need to revisit your literature review as you identify new areas.

Discourse analysis

Data analysis in qualitative desk-based research involves examining what is said or written. Discourse analysis also involves being aware of how things are said, and sometimes even what is not said, either because it has been implied, omitted or even ignored. The focus of this approach is on language and how it is used. Language is a powerful tool in communication and can be used for good or otherwise. Discourse analysis, therefore, is often linked with issues of power in society and it is good to remember that those in power often (even usually) want to keep hold of it. Power dynamics are an important aspect of reflexivity (Fook and Askeland, 2006), and many researchers in the social sciences seek to challenge the misuse of power, especially in relation to inequality and people on the margins of society. Discourse analysis involves looking carefully at words and phrases, including such things as intonation and omissions.

EMMA'S RESEARCH: DISCOURSE ANALYSIS WITH THEMATIC ANALYSIS

I've found a number of TV documentaries online and have decided to focus on a series of four programmes broadcast by the BBC called *Boys Banged Up*. Set in Northern Ireland, it gives an uncompromising view of the lives of young offenders in Hydebank and their lives both inside and outside the institution. I'm particularly interested in the renaming of Hydebank in 2015 as a secure training college and hope the programmes will give me insights on rehabilitation and reoffending.

I've watched the four programmes in sequence to get an overview of the main messages contained within them. What an eye-opener – the lives of the young people are so complex and their circumstances seem so difficult. I've made lots of notes in my research journal as I've been watching them. Sometimes it can be quite difficult to hear what some of the young people are saying – thank goodness for subtitles! Two particular themes are starting to stand out – growing up in poverty and the impact of mental health issues. I'm watching them again now and I need to pause them often to write more detailed notes under these two headings. I've also started drawing a mind map to show the links between aspects of the two main themes with a number of sub-themes.

Figure 11.3 shows Emma's early mind map.

While watching the programmes, Emma has become aware of the way things are said as well as what is actually said. In particular, she is struck by one of the very first comments made by a member of the public in the first programme: 'We are better than those people', said in a very derogatory tone. This speaks

Figure 11.3: Emma's mind map for data analysis

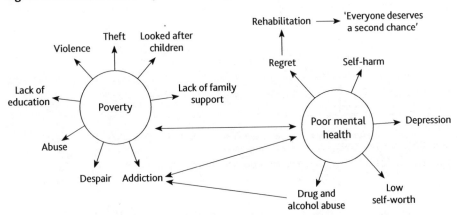

'We are better than those people'

to Emma of issues of power and the way society looks down on certain people, including young offenders.

Emma reads through all her notes and highlights a number of negative comments made about the young people and how they are said. She also reads reviews of the programmes in some prominent newspapers which also contain similar negative comments such as 'They're only sorry for their actions because they got caught.' To Emma this comment contrasts sharply with one of a local councillor who says 'Everyone needs a second chance' and Emma decides to note down comments made about the young people in two columns: one for positive comments and one for negative. She becomes particularly interested in the negative comments and sees these as projecting very negative messages about young people to wider society.

Emma now feels that she has lots of data from the programmes and she knows that this will be too much for her dissertation. She realises that she needs to select the themes that relate most closely to her research question, so goes back to revisit them, thereby engaging with the Research Triangle (see Chapter 1). She amends her overarching question from 'What factors affect people who reoffend?' to 'What factors affect young people who reoffend?' and while she feels issues of poor mental health are significant, she begins to see these as more of a symptom than an underlying reason. She feels that poverty is the root cause of many of these factors and redraws her mind map (see Figure 11.4).

Figure 11.4: Emma's second mind map for data analysis

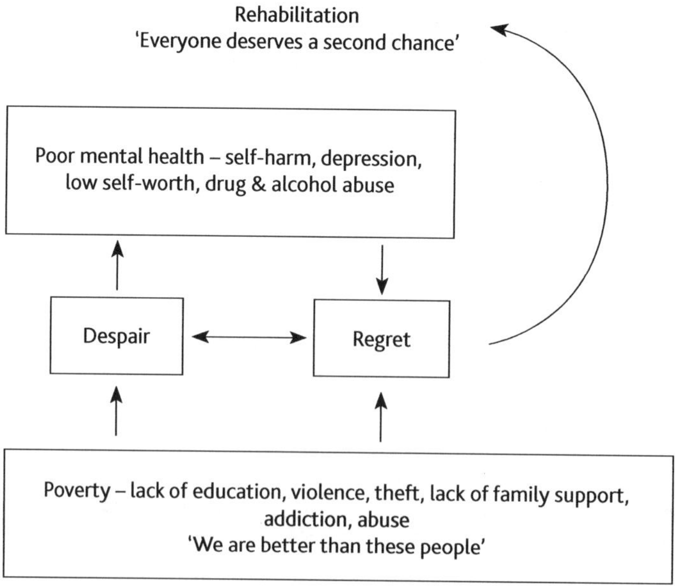

From here she is able to focus on the negative language used in the programmes, in the reviews and in media more widely to show how young offenders are often perceived. She begins to contrast this with information and stories contained in the charity websites she is also examining, where overall the language is distinctly more positive. She goes back to the table with comments made about young people and is able to add several more to the column containing ones that are positive. This table starts to act as a simple coding mechanism that Emma is happy with.

Researchers invariably find they can't include all their data when writing up their study. Difficult decisions have to be made and often interesting data has to be set to one side. This can sometimes be because it doesn't relate to a research question or because there is simply too much to include. This is always difficult but trying to include everything often leads to an analysis that is weak because it is shallow and fragmented.

 You may well not be able to include all the data gathered in your study. Selecting the most appropriate is all part of the research process.

Using direct quotes from your data brings a study to life and these are the tent pegs that support your Metaphorical Tent. They can help to make specific points in relation to the insights gained from it, but don't rely on them too heavily. Remember it's your analysis of the data that is important, so use direct quotes to support your argument (just as you will in your literature review) and don't slip into thinking that they speak for themselves.

 Like 'peachy quotes' from literature, a short, succinct quote from data can bring a study to life.

How to select the most appropriate way to analyse your data

When thinking about which technique for data analysis to use, Largan and Morris (2019: 253–4) offer some helpful questions to consider. In relation to these, Sam, Rajesh and Emma each selected an appropriate way to analyse their data for the following reasons:

- Sam was interested in the stories about refugees, so chose narrative analysis;
- Rajesh was struck by the number of times particular words and phrases appeared in his data, so chose content analysis;
- Emma was fascinated by the kind of words being used, positive and negative, so undertook discourse analysis;
- all of them combined this technique with thematic analysis.

Once you have selected an appropriate technique, do use it consistently and systematically because this will result in a robust analysis that will stand up well to scrutiny when marked.

Some possible analytical tools

Some people enjoy using technology to help them to analyse their data and if this is you, do feel free to try it. There are some important considerations, not least of which is what does your university offer that you can access without having to pay for it? In addition, what does your supervisor recommend? At the time of writing, the most common program used in qualitative research was NVivo. However, remember too that the software you use regularly has some excellent functions that can help too; for example, the search and find functions in your word processor can help you to see key words easily and the comments boxes in the review function are excellent for highlighting and coding data. If in doubt, keep it simple. You have enough work to do already without giving yourself lots more!

 Be sure to use a programme designed for research and not one for market research. If in doubt, ask your library staff and they will be happy to help you.

Back to literature

By now it might seem to be some time since you carried out the majority of your literature review. The purpose of it was to critically evaluate what has been published already which relates to your research question. Having analysed your data, you need to refer back to your literature review to show how your data supports the arguments people have made already and any differences and gaps. To do this, you can ask some key questions in relation to your literature review:

- Which of the key words that I listed when I did my review (see Chapter 8) have I found in my data?
- Which of the key theories and concepts discussed are evident?
- Are any missing?
- Are there things from my data that I would now expect to find in literature that seem to be missing?

All of these will help you to see clear links between the data you have analysed and the published work of other researchers. The final question in the list is perhaps the most important because it will point you to original aspects in your own study and to further research that could be done on your topic. Both are areas for discussion in your conclusions and recommendations, the final section of your dissertation.

SUMMARY

In this chapter we have focused on data analysis. We have examined the four main techniques used in qualitative research and have seen how Sam, Rajesh and Emma have used them. The analysis process involves care and being able to focus on detail, so it will probably take some time to do it justice. In the next chapter we move on to what is often the final step of the process of writing a dissertation, the conclusion and recommendations.

Further reading

- Lester et al (2020) give a thorough phased approach to thematic analysis with some excellent tips.

12

Writing conclusions
and recommendations

In this chapter we will:

☐ discuss how to write strong conclusions and recommendations in a dissertation – the back of the Metaphorical Tent;

☐ use criteria as a way of undertaking a critical evaluation of the whole research project;

☐ examine Sam, Rajesh and Emma's findings;

☐ discuss how you can identify areas for further research;

☐ think about how to write a good abstract;

☐ identify ways of writing a good title.

We are now reaching the end of Part II and by the end of this chapter, you will have erected the whole of your Metaphorical Tent. The focus at this point is on writing conclusions and recommendations and these will serve to make the ending of your dissertation strong and will help you to finish on a high point. In my view, nobody wants a dissertation that just 'peters out' or equally one that is very predictable, so it is well worth thinking about what your work says that is different, or where it can shed some new light on people's understandings of your topic. Your conclusions and recommendations form the back of your Metaphorical Tent.

How to write strong conclusions and recommendations

First, we need to consider the terms conclusions and recommendations and to see how they might apply to your study. The *Oxford English Dictionary* defines the word conclusion in two different ways and both definitions can help us understand what makes a strong conclusion in a dissertation.

1. The end of an event or something finishing – here they point to the need to sum up an argument or text.

2. A judgement or decision reached through reasoning – this is an opportunity for you to put forward your own interpretation based on the thorough analysis of your data.

Some dissertations, especially those written in the applied social sciences, will also include recommendations. These will often relate to further development of research, policy and professional practice in the area being studied.

Although a strong final section will include a summary, it will be much more than that. It will also contain a discussion of your key findings and will be an opportunity for you to offer your own interpretation of the current situation and to give some detail regarding new insights you have gained. So, what makes up a strong conclusions and recommendations section? Thomas (2017: 298) identifies the following six key areas to be included and some of these point to aspects of the definitions discussed in the previous paragraph.

1. A brief summary of the project (as in the first part of the definition).
2. Revisiting the background – this will include a discussion of your research question and sub-questions and how far you reached in gaining new insights into your area of interest. It might be some time since you have looked at these in any detail and doing this now gives you an opportunity to make any final slight modifications to them. A discussion of your research question gives you the opportunity to look back and evaluate what you have found in relation to each aspect. Writing about this can form a large part of a summary of your overall arguments and will make the final section clear, offering a coherent ending to the whole piece, without leaving any loose ends.
3. Evaluating your 'solution' – here you can discuss the conclusions you are able to draw from the analysis of your data. Remember that qualitative research can give valuable insights rather than solutions to problems and be sure to keep your language tentative (see Table 8.2). You can discuss what your research confirms and where it can point to some different understandings.
4. Limitations – all research has limitations and desk-based research is no exception to this. Here you can reflect on your decision to carry out desk-based research and how appropriate this was. You can also discuss how doing empirical qualitative research might have been different and what you might have gained doing your study in this way. You can reflect on things that didn't go according to plan, the changes you made and what you learned from this.
5. Recommendations for further research – all research points to further research as new insights and possibilities emerge. You might want to discuss things like drawing on different data resources and the possibility of developing research questions that have a different emphasis based on what you have found.
6. Implications and recommendations for policy and practice – if your final sub-question leads you nicely into some recommendations, it is good to make this clear here. Again, be sure to make your language tentative as you

make suggestions of how your work could be taken forward. Nobody is impressed by a small-scale project that makes grand claims that are clearly unrealistic.

Thomas' third point shows the need to include a discussion of the insights into your research question that you have gained. Keeping a focus on this will make your conclusions clear and mean that the reader is not left with any 'loose ends'.

Using criteria to write a strong critical evaluation of your study

As part of the final section of your dissertation, you will probably need to include a critical evaluation of what you did, reflecting on how your project developed and what you might do differently if you were beginning again. Some students are asked to write a reflective account on the research process as a separate piece of assessed work, while others are expected to do this as part of the final section of their dissertation. Either way, Tracy's (2010) eight 'Big-Tent' criteria are a very useful tool for doing this and here is a summary adapted for a qualitative desk-based study:

1. Worthy topic – the topic is relevant, timely, significant and interesting.
2. Rich rigour – the study has a strong theoretical underpinning and takes a thorough and clearly articulated approach to data collection and analysis.
3. Sincerity – the researcher takes a reflexive approach in relation to their values and biases and makes their position in the research clear.
4. Credibility – the study contains thick description and is triangulated effectively.
5. Resonance – the research speaks clearly to an audience and has an impact on them.
6. Significant contribution – the research provides some key new insights.
7. Ethical – relevant ethical principles have been applied with integrity.
8. Meaningful coherence – the study achieves what it set out to achieve and there is a strong connection between the research question, literature, data and conclusions.

(Adapted from Tracy, 2010)

When writing an evaluation of your study, you could also reflect on each part of the Metaphorical Tent and how you have constructed it. Here are some questions to help you do this:

- Tent poles – how effective were your research questions and would you want to change them if you did the study again?
- The canvas on the right-hand side (your literature review) – are there other areas of literature you would now want to examine?

- The groundsheet (methodology) – would you still choose to do a desk-based study, or use a different approach?
- The canvas on the left-hand side (your data) – would you now use different data sources?

Writing an evaluation might prompt you to return to a section or two, to continue to refine them. Don't be afraid to do this but remember that it is probably not a good idea to make any major changes at this late stage unless you feel they are absolutely necessary.

 Writing an evaluation is not the time for 'If only I had ...' but rather for 'What I've learned from this is ...'

Sam, Rajesh and Emma's findings

We start by looking at Sam's findings from his narrative analysis.

SAM

I've been so moved by the stories of refugees in my data that I've decided to write a fictional account of a refugee in order to draw together the four key themes from my data. This is the outline of the story and I've written it in three parts.

Part 1 (beginning) – escape from violent conflict
I guess my story began when I was very young, so young it's difficult to remember the detail and, to be honest, I'm grateful for that. Dad had gone off to fight in the civil war that was wrecking our country and Mum was left to look after us all on her own. She often tells us about how things got worse and worse and one day she decided it was time to go. We fled, not knowing where we were going or even if we would survive. There just wasn't a choice. As we headed to the border, we met people along the way. People were saying that they thought there was somewhere safe further on, so we just kept going.

Part 2 (middle) – refugee camp
What a relief it was to see the refugee camp up ahead! Having spent days walking and hoping, to see it there was amazing and we thought we could be safe again. But life in the camp was hard. There were some tents, but not enough for everyone, and food and clean water were in very short supply. There was talk of violence in

---

the camp as people struggled to survive. It was especially hard in the winter as the temperature plummeted below freezing point. We stayed for several months, but Mum knew that we needed to move on if we could in order to survive. One day she decided that we needed to leave. She'd heard of people heading for Europe for a better life and some people talked about going to the US to join their relatives. One night we set off, taking everything we had with us, hoping for the best and feeling very scared. We walked and walked, mostly at night, and hiding to get some sleep during the day. We were tired and hungry but knew we had to keep going. Finally, we got to the coast where we waited to catch a boat to carry us to a safer place. The water was rough, and the sea crossing was very scary.

Part 3 (continuation of challenges) – life in a new country

We landed safely and spent the beginning of our new life in a centre waiting to claim asylum. Would we be accepted? Would they send us back? Thankfully they believed our story and eventually decided we could stay. That was just the beginning though. It took a long time to get accommodation and we had so little to live on. Now we've been here for a number of years, what would I say refugees need? Mum remembers the trauma of it all and I'm sure if she could get some more counselling that would help. She's had a bit, but not enough. It was hard settling into school and nobody really seemed to understand what we went through. There were older boys and girls in school who had been through similar things and they would have been great mentors for us. Mum always says one of the hardest things was finding a job. She was a skilled worker in our country, but her qualifications didn't really count here. It took her ages to get good advice on retraining. Most of all, everyone found learning a new language really difficult and we could all have done with more help here.

RAJESH

I'm now working through my interpretation of my data analysis and the conclusions I'll be able to draw from it. I love the words 'trickle down' that the community-based music therapist used in the podcast and they've really stayed in my mind. I think they're very significant for my study and make me think of water flowing down a stream. I'm going to use this image as a key concept in my conclusions and I've drawn a diagram to help me visualise it.

Figure 12.1 shows Rajesh's diagram.

Figure 12.1: Rajesh's conceptual framework for his conclusions

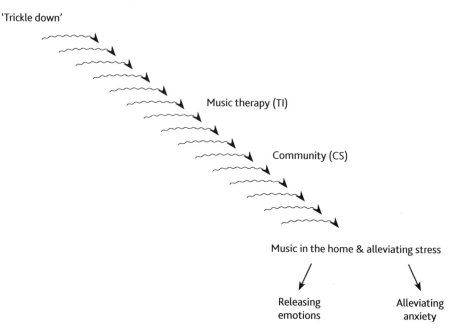

'Trickle down'

Music therapy (TI)

Community (CS)

Music in the home & alleviating stress

Releasing emotions

Alleviating anxiety

Rajesh's research has shown him that the traditional role of music therapists is with individuals. But conceptualising his study in this way helps him to see a clear strategic role for music therapists in the community in bringing more music into people's homes to alleviate their anxieties. Rajesh feels he has something different to say about the role of music therapists and other musicians in promoting music in the home as a means of releasing emotions and alleviating anxiety, something that resonates with the content of the comedian's podcasts.

EMMA

I'm now thinking about my conclusions and recommendations and I'm going to use my second mind map (Figure 11.4) as a tool to help me. I suppose I see it as a cycle from poverty in its various guises as one of the root causes of youth offending, which leads to despair and its associated mental health issues. This often (but not always) leads to regret, which can lead to more despair. I think I need to discuss how the cycle can be broken so regret can be used more positively and lead on to rehabilitation. The positive language of the charities' websites is very helpful here, and in particular the effect mentoring can have. I'm going back to my final sub-question to amend it to focus on how mentoring can support young offenders in the process of rehabilitation.

Writing a good abstract

Writing an abstract is one of the final things you will have to do when completing your dissertation and it is best left to the end. An abstract is designed to provide a summary of the whole piece for the reader. If you think back to all those journal articles you read as part of your literature review, you no doubt read lots of abstracts that helped you to decide whether or not you wanted, or needed, to read the whole article. This is at the heart of the purpose of an abstract. Many students ask me if an abstract is meant to include their conclusions; they often feel that they don't want to disclose these from the very beginning. But my response to this is always yes. Of course, the people marking your work don't have the luxury of deciding whether or not they want to read the whole thing – it's their job! Writing a dissertation is an academic discipline and who knows what you might go on to write next in your academic or professional life?

An abstract needs to be relatively short and, as a general rule, it is best if it fits on to a single page, otherwise it may well be too long. It needs to include the following:

- an initial sentence or two on the topic and something about its importance;
- a short statement of the particular things you were exploring and wanting to find out more about;
- a short, pithy summary of what you did and how you did it, from the beginning of your study to completion;
- some summary points that state what your study shows.

Some key words to include are likely to be examination, qualitative, desk–based, study and insights.

An abstract should always be written in the third person and in the past tense because your study is now complete. Most of all it needs to be concise. Many students find writing an abstract difficult for a number of reasons, not least of which is the level of fatigue they are probably experiencing at the time. It almost always is the very last part of their dissertation that they write – and it should be.

 It is very easy to forget that you need to write an abstract and you might only remember you need to do this close to your submission date. It is definitely worth making a note somewhere (for example, in your research journal) to remind you.

Finalising a good title

This can be one of the trickiest things to write and it's definitely worth thinking about this relatively early on in your study. A good title will tempt the reader into your study and make them want to read it. Here are some suggestions of things that make good and not so good titles for qualitative studies (see Table 12.1).

Table 12.1: Good and not so good titles

Good title	Not so good title
An interesting take on the study	Bland description of the study
Rephrasing your research question in an interesting way to show some of your findings	Simply repeating your research question
Contains an open question	Contains a closed question
Concise and pithy	Too long or too short
Gives an indication of the methodology of the study	Gives no indication of the methodology of the study

In a qualitative desk-based study, a good title might sometimes (but not always) include a direct quote from a data resource.

SAM, RAJESH AND EMMA'S TITLES

Sam's title – Beginnings, middles and ends (or more challenges): stories of refugees and their ongoing survival.

Rajesh's title – 'Trickle down': the role of music in the community in alleviating stress and anxiety.

Emma's title – 'Everyone needs a second chance': a study of discourses in youth offending and rehabilitation.

 Make a note of any suitable titles in your research journal as you go along. You may well not remember them later and find yourself thinking something like 'What on earth was that great title I thought of weeks ago?'

SUMMARY

Having discussed the whole area of writing conclusions and recommendations, we have now reached the end of Part II and the step-by-step process of doing your research project and writing your dissertation is complete. You have now erected your Metaphorical Tent. In Part III we move on to focus on two general themes: getting the support you need and managing your project. Both of these will be important throughout your research project and in keeping your Metaphorical Tent stable and secure.

Further reading

- Becker (2015) offers very helpful advice on writing what she calls 'magnificent conclusions'.

PART III

Keeping your tent stable and secure

Having worked through each step of the process of carrying out a research project, you have now erected your Metaphorical Tent. In Part III we move on to a consideration of more general issues that will help you throughout your research with the ultimate aim of writing a dissertation you can be proud of. Two main areas are included: getting the support you need and making good use of it, and the overall area of managing a desk-based research project. We hear about Sam, Rajesh and Emma's progress as they complete their studies and graduate successfully.

13

Getting the support you need

In this chapter we will:

☐ discuss the role of supervision in your research project and how to get the most from it;

☐ discuss how to use feedback to enable your academic development;

☐ think about the role of a critical friend;

☐ discuss the value of a study group;

☐ consider how you can tap into other types of support offered centrally by your university;

☐ think about how to get the support of others when managing stress.

The focus of this chapter is on making sure you are getting the various types of support you will need as you progress. We all need support in life generally, particularly when we are facing big tasks and challenging issues. Knowing who to go to, and then being sure to get the support, is always better than burying your head in the sand and hoping everything will go away or that everything will be okay in the end. It might be, but on the other hand it might not; having worked hard to get to this point, it's not worth putting your dissertation at risk.

The role of supervision

At some point during the process (for example, when your proposal has gone through ethical clearance), you will be allocated a supervisor. This person will usually work with you from that point through to the completion of your study when you submit your dissertation. Your supervisor might be someone you know already (for example, a tutor who has taught one of your previous modules) or it could be someone new. It goes without saying that it might be someone you like and feel you can work well with, or otherwise. Either way building a positive relationship with them can only enhance your chances of success.

Supervisors are allocated to students by programme or module leaders based on a range of criteria, such as:

- their knowledge of your chosen topic;
- their expertise in a particular research method (for example, quantitative, qualitative);
- their experience in a research approach (for example, narrative, discourse analysis, case study);
- their understanding of how to work with students who have learning needs (for example, dyslexia, dyspraxia);
- the relationship they have built with particular students who need more support for personal reasons and that they have developed via the personal academic tutor role;
- they have sufficient time in their workload.

The allocation of supervisors is usually far from random and is not something that students are generally involved in. Inevitably, some students will be happy when they hear who their supervisor is, and others won't. The most important thing at this point is to build as good a relationship as you can with whoever your supervisor is in order to get the most benefit from their support and knowledge.

Supervision can be a confusing term, especially if you think of it in the context of paid work. A supervisor at work will usually tell you what to do and will then check that you've done it and in the way you were asked. This is very different from supervision in research. So, what does the term supervision mean in this context? Research supervisors play multiple roles; they act as:

- a guide – they have lots of experience, so will be able to help you to see the way forward;
- a mentor – they will 'walk alongside you' in the research process and will discuss things with you;
- a source of information – they are knowledgeable about university systems and processes, as well as your topic, research and resources more generally;
- a facilitator – they help you to get the most from your research, make things easier, but will challenge you too;
- an enabler – they will help you to see how you can make progress and reach your goals.

Understanding the role of the supervisor is very important and this can help you to think about how you can work together effectively. Managing your own expectations is one key element of this, in order to avoid disappointment. Table 13.1 highlights some of the things that a good supervisor will and will not do.

How supervisors work with their students varies from university to university. Many supervisors work with students on an individual level while others work with small groups. Some start with group meetings because in the early part of the process lots of students have similar queries; this saves time and is a way of ensuring that everyone gets important messages at the same time and in the same way. This avoids things being said like 'I wish I'd known that', or 'If only

Table 13.1: The role of a good supervisor

A good supervisor will:	A good supervisor will not:
Treat you with respect	Treat you disrespectfully
Want you to achieve to your full potential	Want you to fail or get a mark lower than you deserve
Guide you through the process of doing your research	Tell you what to do
Offer you support and encouragement	Nag you or remind you of what you need to do, especially when this is clear in relevant and accessible documentation
Offer sessions to individuals and/or groups at a scheduled time and in a designated place	Be able to see you only when and where it suits you, or be at your 'beck and call'
Be happy to hear about the progress you are making, or to hear when you are stuck	Be happy to hear that you haven't done very much work on your study
Want to enable you to study independently	Allow you to become dependent on them
Assume everything is okay if they haven't heard from you	Contact you if you don't reply to their messages
Point you in the right direction for support they are not able to give (for example, from central services)	Answer every little query you might have

I'd known that earlier' or 'They didn't say that to me'. Following some group meetings, they might then move on to hold more individual meetings as time goes on. Whether or not a supervisor chooses to hold some group meetings may well depend on how many students they have been asked to supervise and how much time they have been allocated for this aspect of their work. You might work with your supervisor on an individual level or in a small group and while there may be some scope for negotiation in the way you work with them, this is generally for your supervisor to stipulate and to organise. Students can often feel that individual supervision is better, when in fact group supervision can be really helpful as it gives you the opportunity to learn from your fellow students as well as from the tutor. It also helps you to get to know a small group of students better, leading to more mutual support and can help you to feel less isolated. It is always good to remember that most supervisors are very busy, so their time will be limited.

TIP Qualitative research is often not linear or done in a particular sequence, so be ready to be able to say what kind of support you might need and when. This is especially important if you have a particular learning need.

EMMA

I've just found out who my supervisor is, and I'm gutted! I'd really hoped it would be my favourite tutor who I get on really well with, but they've given me someone I've never even met! Some of my friends have got the tutor I wanted, which makes it even worse. But then I checked on the faculty website and I can see that my supervisor has a real interest in criminology and reoffending. Their published work looks great too, especially one of their recent journal articles. I suppose I'm beginning to realise that they will be in a really good position to support me, so I'm going to contact them as soon as I can to introduce myself and let them know what my research is about.

How to get the most from supervision

The relationship you have with your supervisor will be one of the most important relationships you make during your time at university, so it is good to think about how you will approach this. If you know your supervisor already, it will be about building on the relationship you already have. If you don't, it will be useful to think about how you will approach it. Just like any other working relationship, it will be important to put some time and effort into starting to build it and here are some things you can do that can make a real difference:

- Make the initial contact – some students feel that they need to wait for their supervisor to make the first contact, but this isn't the case. When you know who your supervisor is going to be, make contact with them straight away. They will probably have received a list of all the students they will be supervising and a nice, informal introductory message from you will help to cement you in their minds as one of their new supervisees. It will also save them work, which is always a positive! Replying to a message is always easier and quicker than sending out an initial one. Doing this shows you are well organised, interested and enthusiastic, which is always a good thing; remember, you only get one chance to make a first impression and you want it to be a good one. Sending an initial email will be a good method of communication as they can then reply when they are available. Tell them a bit about your research, how your ideas (including your research questions) have been developing and the things that you have been reading. This means they can see that you are looking ahead and keen to get going. Don't be afraid to send them the latest copy of your research proposal; this will save them time having to look for it.
- Be organised – in Chapter 14 we will discuss the importance of planning and taking an organised approach; this applies to supervision too. Once you have heard from your supervisor, block out the time needed on your schedule for any meetings or individual sessions. If your supervisor holds an initial meeting

(individual or group) try as hard as you can not to miss it; the supervisor will use this to explain how they want to work with you. Be sure to attend and following this, work in the way that they prefer whenever you can. This might include regular email contact, attending group or individual sessions, taking part in recommended sessions provided by central services (for example, literature review, referencing, academic language) and possibly sending them sections of your work for feedback. Supervisors will only suggest things that they know will be helpful to you. They have probably done this many times before and understand what works well. Remember too that refreshing your academic skills is often helpful as well.

- Keep in regular contact – as well as attending supervision sessions, you will probably have some email contact with your supervisor. There are some things to watch here in order to continue to build your positive working relationship and a lot of this is about striking the right balance – so, not too much contact and not too little. Supervisors are busy and can understandably be irritated by lots of short messages. If you know you have several questions to ask, it is better to put them into one longer message than to send several. Try not to ask things that you know you can find out elsewhere. For example, you should be able to find out the answers to administrative issues, such as deadlines, how to submit your work and concessions arrangements fairly easily via your student portal or handbook. If you're having difficulties, you could try asking a fellow student in your group first or an administrator rather than your supervisor.

- Be conscientious in your approach – all supervisors enjoy working with students who take their studies seriously, work hard, meet deadlines and want to do well. Supervisors also like working with students who keep in touch and do what they say they are going to do. They don't like it when students 'go silent on them' and then they have to make the effort to contact them, sometimes multiple times, before they get a response. They particularly don't like it when students leave everything until the last minute and then expect lots of support all at once, close to the submission deadline.

- Be open-minded and flexible – remember, supervisors are there to guide, support and to give you feedback and being open to this is an important part of the supervisory process. They won't tell you what to do and will be happy to see you working independently. However, they will offer advice, and their experience will no doubt mean it will be worth listening to and taking action on.

Universities vary in their expectations of supervisors, including the amount of time they should spend with each student, the proportion of text they can comment on, and whether or not they are allowed to review drafts or only final versions of students' work. It is well worth asking your supervisor about things like this, so you can manage your expectations.

Remember to build a positive relationship with your supervisor by working with them in the ways that suit them.

Supervisors are busy people and their teaching and research commitments mean they will not always be free to respond to you straight away. Most universities have protocols for the maximum amount of time it should take to receive a response to an email, so do make sure you are aware of this and act accordingly. Sending a follow-up email before the maximum time agreed expires will only make their inbox even more clogged up than it already is! This will inevitably mean it will take them longer to reply. From my own personal perspective, a student who also copies in my line manager when sending me a message like this is particularly unwelcome!

 Your supervisor is not a personal friend. Think carefully about the language you use in emails (clear and not too informal). Always use the appropriate channel – your university email not your personal email and not via something like LinkedIn.

How to use feedback to good effect

You will already understand that good feedback is very important for your academic development, and feedback from your supervisor will be key in helping you write an excellent dissertation. At this point it is good to think about how you can use this effectively. Your supervisor will discuss your work with you and will give you feedback as you progress. You might receive feedback from your fellow students too, especially if some of your supervision is done in a group. However, not all feedback is good feedback and having an understanding of this will make you aware of times when you might need to ask for more.

Good feedback is always respectful of your work and is helpful and supportive. This means it is constructive, showing the positives as well as the areas for development and improvement. The development points will be focused and specific, practical and understandable, and will be honest and given with integrity. It will also be timely and in a measured amount, so not all at once and too much to take in (especially if you have maintained regular contact) but not too little either. It will also be timely, not too soon and not too late. Good feedback will help to keep you motivated and working towards achieving the end goal of a dissertation you can be proud of. Table 13.2 shows the characteristics of good and bad feedback.

It's good to remember though that feedback can sometimes be difficult to hear and receive. Working independently means we can easily get into some kind of

Table 13.2: Good and bad feedback

Good feedback	Bad feedback
Respectful of your work	Disrespectful of your work
Helpful and supportive	Accusatory and unhelpful
Builds confidence	Undermines confidence
Constructive	Destructive
Includes positives and development points	Only includes negative criticisms
Measured in amount	Too much to take in at once
Focused and detailed	Too little and woolly
Keeps an open mind	Judgemental

'bubble' where we assume everything is okay, even good, when in fact this might not be the case. Feedback can then come as a bit of a shock if it's not as positive as we thought it would be. In my experience students vary in their expectations and in their responses to feedback. Some students I work with find it difficult to see the positives in their work and expect negative feedback even when their work is actually good. This means they find it difficult to accept positive feedback and praise and are always looking for more to validate their work. This can make them appear lacking in self-confidence. Others assume their work is good (or that it will be) when it might not be as good as they think and so are reluctant to accept any development points, assuming they know best. This can make them appear overconfident and even arrogant. Feedback can help you to see things that you can't otherwise; this is sometimes referred to as the 'blind area' (Luft, 1984). The key message is to know yourself well and looking back on your previous marks and feedback should give you a good indication either way. If your marks have been high and you feel your work might not be good enough, maybe you need to have more confidence in your abilities. If your marks haven't been as good as you would have liked, maybe it's time to start listening to feedback more closely and acting on it. Remember though, it is your work and you are responsible for the decisions you take, including how you respond to feedback and whether or not you choose to take action in the light of it.

 Try not to take feedback too personally. If you feel the feedback you are getting is negative, look for the development points. If they aren't clear, don't be afraid to ask your supervisor for some clarification. It's better to do this than work in the dark.

A good supervisory relationship is built on mutual respect, but this does not mean that feedback is always easy to receive or that you will always agree with the points your supervisor makes. A good supervisor will always want to hear your arguments for your approach and ultimately this will help you when it comes to writing up your work for submission.

SAM

I'm getting quite a lot of feedback, but some of it is really quite hard to take. I'm going to talk to my supervisor about it to see if I should be worried. It feels like my confidence is a bit low at the moment.

My supervisor is great – they went through some of the points and now I can see that most of them are to help make my work even better, while others need more work. Often, it's that I need to add more detail. I'm so close to everything now; it's easy to assume whoever is going to read my work can see the points I'm trying to make, when they probably don't and I need to make them clearer. I've looked back at some of my earlier drafts and I can see definite improvements, so I'm determined to keep going.

The role of a critical friend

While undertaking your research project, you may well find it helpful to work with a critical friend. Critical friendship can be a significant help to our development in a number of ways and unpicking the term reveals some key aspects of it:

- Critical – this word has two meanings. The first is that it is vitally important (for example, critical care) and, second, that it won't always be all positive.
- Friend – a true friend will be unhappy if they are only telling us things we want to hear and not being totally honest with us. A good friend should and will tell us when we don't look so good in that outfit or when we have broccoli in our teeth! A friend will be honest but sensitive to how we feel at the same time.

So, what makes a good critical friend and how should you choose one? A good critical friend is someone who you know already and can trust. Friends do not steal from one another; this applies to ideas and academic work as well as material possessions. They will be a good listener and ready and able to ask questions sensitively to challenge your thinking and your approach. They will act with integrity and always have your interests at heart. They will be positive, constructive and encouraging, always wanting the best for you. They won't shy away from discussing any apparent weaknesses in your research, but will do this in a sensitive questioning way, asking you to explain why you have done things in the way you have. They will also be happy to point out the strengths in your work. The core qualities of a strong critical friendship are similar to those of supervision and include mutual respect and trust, openness, honesty and good mutual understanding.

A supportive and effective critical friend takes a sensitive and questioning approach. They ask open questions, such as 'What made you take that particular approach?' so you have to think things through in a deeper and more critical way.

You may feel you have someone who acts as a critical friend already, but if not, you will want to spend some time thinking about who could do this and to choose them carefully. It is worth remembering that it may well not be your best friend and should be someone who you know will ask you challenging questions. In the long run, this will be much more helpful than someone who will just say that they think everything is fine as it is when that's not really what they think and they don't feel able to be more honest with you.

The value of a study group

Studying can be challenging at times and during your time at university you may or may not have become part of a study group. If not, now could be a good time to consider joining one or even making one happen. A group like this can be very helpful in a number of ways:

- you have access to support from fellow students when things might get tough, which can be particularly helpful as deadlines loom and stress levels can rise;
- you can compare notes from supervision sessions;
- you can share your understanding of key research concepts;
- you can share resources (for example, research methods books);
- you can learn from each other as you will all have different strengths and weaknesses;
- you have good opportunities for discussion in a non–threatening environment.

The size and makeup of a study group is important in order for it to be most effective. Many people agree that a good size is four to six students, and it works best if everyone is studying on the same or similar programme. However, triads (or groups of three) can work very well too. There must be a high level of trust between group members and everyone needs to be committed to the group. Everyone needs to get on well and enjoy spending time together; we all learn more when we are having some fun! Study groups are often informal, and you will need to discuss what works best for those in the group. Students living on or near the university campus can afford to be flexible in their approach, for example, spending an hour together, going off to study separately and then getting back together again later to discuss what they have achieved. This can really help with keeping everyone motivated. Those living at some distance will welcome more regular meetings at particular times of the day when everyone can attend. In all cases it will be important to make sure that no one misses out. Importantly, you will also need to be clear about what the goals of the group are, so that meetings are purposeful.

An effective group meeting will usually last no longer than two hours and may be shorter. Finding a good place to meet will be important too and many university libraries contain rooms you can book in advance for study group meetings. Others have open areas where groups can meet more informally. Meeting online via your VLE or Zoom will also be a good option for many. It is always important to be a good member of a study group and nobody wants to be in a group which is dominated by one person who talks all the time. Also, people justifiably get upset if someone doesn't 'pull their weight' and just takes all the time without giving anything back to the group. Equally, it is very frustrating if someone regularly doesn't turn up and doesn't let anyone know that they aren't coming. Being part of a study group will help you to build some more close friendships with people you can call on and these may well be some of the people you celebrate with on graduation day!

Accessing other types of support

Being in the final year at university can be challenging and many of us will need people around who can help us. You may well already be aware of the different types of support available, but here is a reminder:

- Personal support – this will usually be provided by a tutor with a title such as Personal Academic Tutor (PAT) or Personal Tutor and hopefully you will have had some contact with them already. This person is your first 'port of call' if you get into any kind of difficulties.
- Central services – these include counselling or wellbeing, accommodation and finance who can offer you more specialised support if needed.
- Your Programme Director or Course Leader – this person has the overall academic responsibility for your programme and can help with more general queries. If things become very difficult and you are considering interrupting your studies, it is well worth contacting them. At this late stage it would definitely be a mistake just to drift and drop out as you have too much to lose.
- General academic support – this is often available via your VLE and there may be dedicated study support staff in the library who you can ask too.
- Library staff – are invariably very helpful and enjoy responding to more complex queries (for example, in relation to your literature search).

- IT support – again staff here are helpful, so don't worry about asking even basic questions if you need to.
- Disability support – it will be just as important in these final stages to make full use of this if it is available to you, as it was in the first few months of your studies. If you've lost contact, don't be afraid to get back to them to ask for the support you need.

Most universities have systems in place to help students who have personal difficulties, and the general rule is that if you don't seek help and support, staff will assume that everything is okay.

Many students experience difficulties through no fault of their own when unexpected life events simply intervene. If you are having personal difficulties and need help, always be proactive and seek it out. It's definitely a mistake to struggle on your own – all staff want to support students to complete their studies successfully.

If you're having difficulties, don't struggle on your own. Reach out for support.

RAJESH

I had a call the other day from one of my close friends and they can see that my anxiety levels are rising as the deadline for submitting my dissertation is getting nearer. We usually have a meal, relax and watch a film together and they've noticed that I'm tending to miss these times, saying that I'm too busy. They suggested having a coffee instead and I said yes, because I felt I needed a break. Over coffee my friend said they were worried about my mental health and encouraged me to contact the person I know in student wellbeing again for a chat. I really appreciate their friendship and am so glad they are looking out for me. I contacted student wellbeing the next day and got an appointment.

Getting the support of others to help you to manage stress

We all need *some* stress in our lives because it keeps us motivated. But too much stress causes distress, which can hamper our progress, and it is good to remember our own self-care as discussed in Chapter 10. As part of this it is good to consider who would be able to support you if you should need it, and this is where family and close friends become even more important to us than usual. Keeping in regular contact and having a chat with people we know well can help us to relax and take our mind off things. These special people in our lives will also encourage us to keep working and prompt us to get back to work if we need it! Everyone needs a proper break of some kind at some point, so scheduling a visit home or time out with friends for a meal or to see that new film can be really helpful. But equally, none of us should feel under pressure to do things we don't want to do or that we feel we don't have time for at the moment. Things can usually be delayed to a time in the not-too-distant future when you will be able to relax and enjoy them even more.

SUMMARY

This chapter has focused on making sure you have the support you need from people around you. This includes your supervisor and other university staff, other students and family and friends. It is good to remember that people around us won't necessarily always know how we feel and that we may well need to ask for help when we need it. In the final chapter we will move on to consider the whole area of managing your research project successfully.

Further reading

- Evans (2007) includes a short chapter (Chapter 6) on maximising the benefits of supervision.
- Roberts and Seaman (2018) provide a clear discussion on the characteristics of good supervision and some of the potential difficulties.

14

Managing desk-based research

> In this chapter we will:
>
> ❐ discuss the whole area of managing your research project, including planning, goal setting and effective time management;
>
> ❐ consider how to deal effectively with any difficulties you might have;
>
> ❐ examine the practical aspects of good project management;
>
> ❐ help you to reassess your motivation for your research;
>
> ❐ discuss some general strategies for managing stress;
>
> ❐ look forward to your graduation.

In this final chapter we will examine a wide range of issues related to managing your research project. Some universities use the term independent study to describe a dissertation module (see Chapter 6) and this usefully describes how you need to approach it. It is something that you do independently, with support. Studying independently is something that you will have learned how to do since starting your degree, but here, in what is probably the final stage of your undergraduate studies, it is even more important that you can do this effectively. This means taking control of your project and managing it well for yourself. While there will be deadlines to meet along the way, such as dates for sending draft sections to your supervisor and, of course, a final submission date, how you organise and plan your work will be down to you; nobody else will do this for you and indeed they shouldn't.

Your dissertation may well be significantly longer than any other piece of assessed work you have submitted already on your course. There are different ways of dealing with this, but many students I work with find it helpful initially to think of it as writing two or three pieces of work for their modules (depending on how long the dissertation is and the number of credits it attracts – see Chapter 6) rather than one long piece. This can make a real difference, reducing what can initially appear as a huge and potentially daunting task into something much more manageable. It can then begin to feel like something they have done before and achieved.

Planning your project

In many ways, planning your project is key for your success. You may remember the phrase 'to fail to plan is to plan to fail' and there is a lot of truth in this. At university there is always support at hand, so please be ready to ask for it. There is certainly no shame attached to doing this and in my experience, especially in these final stages, academic staff would far rather students ask for help than struggle on their own, or even worse, fail to submit their work at all, putting their whole degree in jeopardy. As discussed in Chapter 2, all of this really is excellent preparation for future work where you will often be expected to show initiative and manage your own workload without close supervision.

Here are some key ways that you can start to plan your research project. A good first step is to devise an initial plan by working back from your submission date. In Chapter 2 we saw how Emma did this. Keeping the final deadline in mind will give you a sharp focus and whatever happens you will want to avoid submitting your work late without applying for extenuating circumstances and incurring a penalty. Doing this is never worth it, but in my experience a very small number of students somehow seem to lose sight of this. When writing any assignment, it is always easier to get the first few marks than the last few, so you are highly unlikely to get a higher mark by submitting your work late and incurring a penalty than by submitting it as it is by the deadline.

As discussed in Chapter 6, your dissertation is a large piece of work, so it is good to break it down into its component parts. In time management literature this is often referred to as the 'salami method' (Tracy, 2017; Bliss, 2018). As we know, a salami is a large sausage that is usually eaten in thin slices. Writing a good dissertation is usually not something you can achieve in one go, so you will need to break it down to make it doable. You can use the salami method to make a detailed plan which can help you to start work in good time and to construct a study schedule.

Starting with the deadline date and working back from it is a good way to plan your research project. Then you can work out how many weeks there are between now and that date; working back from the submission date means you should be able to make a provisional plan of what you need to do and by when. Here, the word provisional is important as any plan you make will need to be flexible. A weekly plan often works well, as this breaks things down into manageable 'chunks'. You could try using your dissertation guidance or handbook as an outline to map out what you will aim to do week by week. Remember to include time to look at data resources and for analysing your data. You may be offered sessions to review research methods and you will also want to factor in your supervision sessions. You will also need time for your literature search and independent reading, and for the final writing up. Working ahead of the final deadline will allow you enough time for editing, making corrections and proofreading your work. As the deadline approaches you may well want to make a plan leading up to the day to make sure you don't miss anything.

Most students find they need to review their plan as their project moves on, so they continue to make progress. It simply isn't possible to anticipate everything, and equally it can be very difficult to estimate how long each aspect will take. Sometimes things might take more or less time than you think, so any plan you make needs to be reviewed and adjusted regularly. Effective planning also means knowing yourself well and being able to respond to such questions as:

- How do I manage deadlines? Some people work best when the deadline is far ahead because it prevents panic setting in. Panic can often mean that concentrating becomes very difficult and, when it becomes intense, immobilisation can happen and at its worst it can feel impossible to do anything. If this sounds like you, you will need to plan well ahead. But other people do their best work when the deadline is relatively imminent because this is when they are in the flow, their adrenalin is running high and they are focused. As an academic and a supervisor, I really don't want to say it's okay to leave everything to the last minute! But do use all the time you have to best effect.
- When do I do my best work? Again, people are different and work differently. Some work best in the morning and others through the night. Some work best in short spurts with regular breaks while others just like to keep going. I know for myself that I work best in the morning, especially when I am writing a book like this. By lunchtime I will be flagging, so I then need to do something that is less demanding. When I was writing my doctoral thesis, I soon realised that writing in the morning and spending the afternoon reading and planning for the next day worked very well for me. This meant I could get going again quickly the next day because I knew what I was doing. I relaxed in the evening, so I didn't become overtired, and took time off at the weekend. Writing about this here sounds easy – believe me, it wasn't!
- How do I like to structure my studies? Many people like to work on a task in a step-by-step way from start to finish because it gives a clear structure, a sense of making progress and ultimately a real feeling of achievement. However, when it comes to qualitative research, this often won't work well and could at times even be a hindrance. For example, if you try and write a full introduction as a starting point, it can often be very difficult. The first and last sentences or paragraphs in any piece of written work are very often the most difficult things to write and it is easy to get completely stuck, so leaving them until later often works better. Most people would say you should always leave writing an abstract (which typically goes at the very beginning of your dissertation, see Chapter 12) to the very end. The nature of qualitative research also means that we often need to work on more than one thing in any given period of time. Looking back at the Research Triangle in Chapter 1 is useful at this point, as it is a reminder of the need to revisit and refine your research question, continue to engage with reading relevant literature and analyse the data you have collected in an ongoing and iterative way. An introduction should include your research question and sub-questions (those 'tent poles'

that support your Metaphorical Tent); writing a final draft of this very early in the process only then to find you have to go back and amend it several times will be disappointing. So, think about the order in which you will write the various sections and be ready to dip in and out of each of them as you progress.

- How do I manage my life outside my studies? Some of us have busier lives and more responsibilities than others, and all of us need to take an honest look at what we have to deal with day by day to maintain a healthy work–life balance. Our everyday lives don't stop just because we are writing a dissertation, so whether it's paid work, family or other commitments, be sure to factor these into your plans.
- How long does it generally take me to do things? By now you may well have an idea how long it takes you to do something like write an essay or read a challenging journal article and this knowledge should act as a useful guide. If not, do look back to the work you did in the previous semester or academic year and try to calculate roughly how long it took you. Often people find they have a tendency to either over- or underestimate the time it will take them to do something. I know for myself that I always underestimate how long something will take, so much so that I now make a plan and double the time!

 TIP **Before you finish writing on a particular day, write a few words of what you are moving on to next, maybe a sentence or two. When you come back to it, it will be much easier to remember what you were going to write next and to start where you left off.**

Drucker apparently once said 'Plans are just good intentions unless they immediately degenerate into hard work' and there is a lot of truth in this. I have known people plan and plan again, but then do very little to move their work forward. In particular, if you have a strong Pragmatist learning style (Honey and Mumford, 2000) you might love planning so much that you will spend far too much time on it to the detriment of taking any action and getting on with the task in hand. If this sounds like you, it is probably time to focus on developing your Activist learning style, so you don't lose too much time. A fantastic plan for a dissertation doesn't on its own make a fantastic dissertation!

In his Management by Objectives Model, Drucker (1954) puts forward a framework that could be a useful planning tool. Written for business, it has been adapted here for the context of a qualitative desk-based research project. It involves the following five steps:

- Review your overall progress – think about what you are hoping to achieve.
- Look back at your research question and sub-questions – make sure they are guiding the focus of your work.

- Monitor your own progress – ask yourself how far you have come and what you still need to achieve.
- Evaluate your performance so far – think about how well you are doing and the areas where you feel you could do better.
- Reward yourself – give yourself a boost with some kind of treat.

Allen's (2015) four-criteria model can also be helpful in the planning process and the four criteria are as follows:

- Context – what can I do here? Think about your own study, work and personal context and try and take a practical and objective view of what you can realistically do.
- Time available – what time do I have now? Think about the time you have day by day and week by week and how you will use it to best effect.
- Energy available – how much energy do I have at the moment? This goes back to thinking about when you work best and using this time to your greatest benefit.
- Priority – what are the most important tasks that need to be done now? Prioritising is an essential part of time management and while it might be lovely to read more, as time goes on, writing has to become more important. You will need to reassess your priorities regularly during the research process.

Having a detailed plan is usually a positive thing, but even experienced researchers say that research projects rarely go completely smoothly. It is often the case that a desk-based project will be more predictable than an empirical study, but this does not mean that life in general is always predictable! It is good to think of your project plan as a working document that you amend as and when you need to, so it will remain useful as your study progresses. In my experience, the most common reasons why things don't go according to plan are personal reasons that can't be avoided. Life can always throw something at us when we least expect it; significant illness and bereavement are two examples. At times like this, do make your supervisor aware of your situation as soon as possible. Also, be sure to access all the support you can from other sources (see Chapter 13) and apply for an extension to the deadline for extenuating circumstances when appropriate. It can be very frustrating when things don't go according to plan, but being flexible and keeping the end goal in mind will help you to build resilience in the face of the immediate challenges.

But does planning always work? Planning is generally a positive thing, but it also has some disadvantages, especially if you stick to it too rigidly. Two particular things are worth bearing in mind: first, because you are probably carrying out your study over quite a long period of time, your motivation will inevitably fluctuate. At certain times you might feel more like doing certain things rather than others. This can mean that at a particular point in time you might not feel like doing whatever is on your plan. If you decide to stick to your plan, you may then not achieve as much and fall behind as a result. At times like this it is often better to be flexible and do the things you feel like doing, as you will probably make more progress. However, most of us like certain aspects more than others and it will be important not to leave everything you dislike or find difficult to the end. This could well lead to a hard slog as the deadline approaches.

Occasionally a student has said to me that planning does not help them; in fact, it hinders them. This can be the case, especially if you have particular learning needs (for example, certain types of dyslexia). If this applies to you, you will probably find it better to use your experience so far and to work in the way that suits you best. However, if your strategies stop working at any point, always remember to access the learning support that hopefully has been organised for you.

Think about where you keep your plan so you have it ready to hand. Your research journal is one obvious place and some students find it helpful to put it on a large sheet of paper above their computer, as a visual reminder. You could also scan it and send it to your university email address, so you have it on your smartphone or tablet. This means you will always have a copy of it in case you need to refer to it, or if you happen to lose it.

 Keep your plan somewhere where you can refer to it easily.

Goal setting

Goal setting is a common technique used when managing all kinds of different projects and can also be useful when managing a research project. You might have used this technique before or intended to use it but have not got round to it. Equally you might have tried it in the past with varying levels of success. One of the most significant benefits of doing this is that it can give a real sense of purpose and achievement. If we don't know what we want and need to achieve, we won't have a sense of direction, and can then feel that we are not making progress and even a bit lost.

Goals can be long term (for the duration of your research project), medium term (for the next month) and short term (for the coming week or even the day itself). Many agree that goals need to be SMART:

- Specific – if they are too general, they may not give us a clear sense of direction or purpose. They also need to contain a level of detail to be helpful with clear tasks identified.
- Measurable – we need to be able to measure the progress we are making towards achieving them.

- Achievable – we need to know that we can achieve them. Setting goals that we know we are unlikely to achieve is very demotivating and can make us feel like giving up altogether. But goals need to be challenging too; if we can achieve them too easily, they may not stretch us, and we might end up doing less than we would otherwise.
- Realistic – we need to be honest with ourselves when setting goals; this goes back to knowing ourselves and what we can and can't do in any given period of time. If we set goals that can only be achieved in an ideal world, we probably won't achieve them, which is very disheartening.
- Time-scaled – deadlines are important reminders to keep our progress in check and help us with the constant battle against procrastination. Often, when studying independently we will need to set our own interim deadlines as part of the process of monitoring our own progress.

RAJESH

I know I need to set myself some clear goals to keep myself motivated and to reduce my levels of anxiety. My project is coming to an end and I'm determined to meet the submission deadline. I just need to keep writing and checking everything is here that's meant to be. It really feels like I'm almost there.

Effective time management

Planning and goal setting are two important elements of time management but there are other areas that are worth considering too. Three other key themes in time management literature are dealing with procrastination, coping with interruptions and understanding the difference between the important and the urgent.

1. Procrastination is commonly referred to as 'the thief of time'. This is because, as we put off doing things, the time we have disappears and it is as if it has been stolen from us. Everyone suffers from procrastination and we can all put off doing things we don't like or find difficult. If you find this is happening to you, one good way to deal with it is to do the thing you have been putting off the most. Many people (including myself) find keeping a 'to-do' list helpful, and I know at times I have to make a point of doing the thing that has been on my list for longest before devising a new one. Often when we do tackle something like this, it's not as difficult as we first thought, and we can get a great sense of achievement from completing it. However, if you're still finding it difficult, be sure to ask for support to overcome whatever barrier it is you are facing.

2. Dealing with interruptions – there are many things that can easily distract us and make us waste a lot of time. Some of these will be very familiar, such as time spent on social media or surfing the internet, chatting with well-meaning friends or checking emails. Whatever it is that you find distracts you, it is well worth trying to do something about it. Putting your phone on silent (or even turning it off) and logging out of email can help a lot. Arranging to meet up with those well-meaning friends at the end of the day or during a break may well mean that you enjoy the time with them more than you would otherwise.

3. Understanding the difference between the important and the urgent – things that are urgent demand our immediate attention (or seem to) and give us the impression that they need to be done right now. Things that are important help us to achieve our long-term goals. Your dissertation is important as it will help you get the degree you want. However, as time goes on and the deadline looms, it will become urgent too. We need to be careful not to spend too much time on urgent things and thereby not enough on the important ones, because the result may well be that we fail to achieve our long-term goals.

One of my own particular phrases is 'the only time I have is the time I make'. I am a busy person and in general I feel my time is pretty full and sometimes too full. So, if I want to achieve something important, I need to make the time for it; it won't just happen on its own. Writing my doctoral thesis was a case in point – something I had to make time for, or it simply wouldn't have happened. This involved putting my studies first when I could, which often meant saying 'no' in a tactful way when people wanted me to do things that I knew I didn't have time for at that particular point. It also meant not being afraid to ask for help and practical support when I needed it.

SAM

I'm struggling again with time management. I've got a clear project plan on my wall, but time seems to be just disappearing. I spoke to my critical friend today who always seems to be well organised and 'ahead of the game'. She tactfully told me that I'm always very quick to reply to emails and that I seem to be on social media sites quite a lot – so much so that I often distract her! I'm going to have a complete break from social media during the day and only check emails at the beginning, middle and end of each day. I think this will really help me to keep a focus and to make more of the time I've got.

Dealing with difficulties to build resilience

We can all experience difficulties when things come up that we don't expect. This can happen in different ways during a research project and it is easy to let these get in the way of the progress we want to make and to feel that we are falling behind. This could even make us feel like we are 'stalling', as it can take time to work out a way forward. It is fair to say that desk-based research is generally more predictable than empirical research, but this doesn't mean that nothing can or will go wrong. Here are two examples of things that can happen that you might not expect and some possible ways of dealing with them:

- Relevant permission is withheld – in Chapter 10 we discussed the importance of trying to get permission to use data resources. In certain situations, people might be happy to give their consent initially and then change their mind. This will mean spending some time finding some alternative data resources.
- Things disappear from the internet – this might sound strange, but sources can be withdrawn from the internet without any prior warning. For example, a film or documentary that you plan to examine as part of your study suddenly disappears without trace. You might be able to find it using the internet archive Wayback Machine (2014) or it might mean finding an alternative source quickly that fulfils a similar function. In any case, it's good not to procrastinate and to be sure to watch it and analyse it early on in your study.

Being flexible and finding alternatives will help you to move forward. Think about what you can still do; it might be that you will have enough data even if some of your sources disappear from the internet. It's always good to see what you can salvage, even if it is only a small part. Another option could be to switch to a literature review or even secondary research; either could offer you a viable alternative. Remember that you may well have done some of the work on these already. A literature review you are in the process of writing or have written could be extended with some work on adjusting your research question and sub-questions. You might already have looked at some published studies as part of your literature review and these could be used as data instead.

 If you feel things aren't going to plan, be sure to talk to your supervisor. They will be able to help you to see an alternative way forward.

Practical aspects of project management

Whatever stage you are at in your qualitative desk-based study it will be important to take a practical approach. This means focusing on tasks (things you need to do and achieve) and wherever possible, not allowing things to build up and subsequently 'mushroom' to the point where they feel out of control. Here are some practical tips to help:

- Try and do things as you go along – this often makes life so much easier than leaving everything to the end. This particularly applies to the mundane and, dare I say, boring bits! I have yet to meet anyone who enjoys collating references and making sure they are in the requested style – I certainly don't. But I know that if I leave everything to the end it will be a mammoth task and so much worse than it would have been if I had kept up with it along the way. The key here is to keep an accurate record and to build it step by step. You might find it useful to use a tool like RefWorks or another online tool, but in my experience, they sometimes only do part of the job and I seem to end up doing a lot of checking. Then it feels like it would have been easier to do them myself anyway.
- Don't be afraid to use what you have already – by this I mean reference lists from your previous assignments. It can be a good idea to put these into one alphabetical list so you can find them easily. It's then much easier to copy and paste them into a new list than doing them all over again.
- Don't forget your appendices – these could include the framework you developed for data analysis or emails you sent to request permissions.
- Keep a close eye on your word count – remember that a good dissertation is a balanced one, so be sure to keep enough words for each section. It can be very tempting to write more in those sections you find easier, but this may well mean that you don't get as high a mark as you would like. If you end up writing far more than your word count allows, trying to trim it down can take a lot of time and you will always risk deleting the best bits.
- Don't get it right, get it written – this was the best piece of advice I received while doing my doctoral study and it can really help if you are suffering from procrastination. Remember we write in order to understand, so keep writing and your understanding will develop (see Chapter 3).
- Check your work for plagiarism – before you submit, be sure to use a plagiarism checker on your portal to avoid any issues.
- Save, save and save again – with most of us working on some kind of cloud system where work is saved automatically, this might sound a bit old-fashioned! But even the best IT system can play some cruel tricks. One example is if we postpone updates and click remind me later. We then forget and before we know it the updates have started and we have lost work; even if it's only a small amount, it can be very disheartening. I still hear stories from students who have somehow 'lost' their work and can't retrieve it. It's always a good idea to save it and send it to your university email address. That way if something happens to your IT account (for example, a data breach), someone in IT services should be able to help you retrieve it.

Reaching the finish line is always a great feeling and in any large project it can be very tempting just to want to get there. However, please be sure to check all the detail; I've lost count of the number of students who have emailed me following submission saying that they have forgotten to include a particular aspect, most commonly their reference list. If you are working ahead of the deadline, this might not be a problem, as you may be able to overwrite your work. But if it's past the deadline when you realise, it could affect your mark adversely.

Reassessing your motivation

Understanding what motivates you will be an important factor in keeping you motivated to ultimately finish your research project. Motivation is an abstract concept and is, therefore, difficult to define, but it usually includes factors and processes that prompt us to do things in certain ways. It also includes what gets in the way and why we fail to do things even though we want to. Many theorists have sought to explain what motivation is and these theories can be put into two main groups: content and process. They often identify factors that motivate people. Some people are motivated by external (extrinsic) factors and some by internal (intrinsic) factors and many of us are motivated by both. Here is an example of each type of motivation theory:

- Maslow's (1954) hierarchy of need – this is probably one of the best-known content theories of motivation. It is usually depicted as a pyramid and asserts that we are motivated to satisfy our basic biological and physiological needs (for example, food and water – extrinsic) at the base of the pyramid before we can satisfy other higher order needs such as self-actualisation (sometimes described as fulfilling our potential – intrinsic).
- Vroom's (1964) expectancy theory – a process theory where the argument is that people make choices based on the reward they expect to receive. People value different outcomes (some extrinsic and some intrinsic) and work in proportion to how much they feel they will achieve. So, people put in a lot of effort if they feel their chances of success are high and vice versa.

In more recent research, Pink (2009) proposes that motivation is made up of three key elements:

- autonomy – having some control over your own work;
- mastery – working at something in detail to get better at it;
- purpose – connecting with a larger vision or goal.

All of these three have a clear role in relation to the motivation needed to complete a research project and write an excellent dissertation.

If you understand more about what motivates you, you should be able to maintain your motivation better and to continue to make progress. Identifying any barriers to motivation will be important too, so that you can take appropriate action to overcome them.

A large-scale project will inevitably have its peaks and troughs and at times you may even feel you have developed a 'love–hate' relationship with it. So, having some coping strategies will always be helpful and at this point it is good to think about how to make the most of the peaks and how to survive the troughs.

Making the most of the peaks should be the easy part and, in many ways, it is. This is a good time to keep going, to take full advantage of the energy and enthusiasm you have and not spend too much precious time thinking about it. In my experience it's all too easy to sit back, relax and lose focus. Before you know it, you have taken your foot off the metaphorical accelerator, slowed down and now feel you are behind. I don't remember any student saying they are finding things difficult because they are so far ahead of where they thought they would be!

Working through the troughs can be much more difficult. At times like this you need to try to keep going, so your study does not come to a complete halt and here are some ideas that might help:

- Take a short break – the word I want to emphasise here is short! Things can sometimes seem very difficult simply because we are tired, so having a relaxing break and a good night's sleep really can help. We then find we have more energy, our concentration is better and we make progress more quickly. This encourages us, and we make even more progress as a result. But taking a long break might have a negative effect as it can be very difficult to get going again.
- Speak to someone – see the sources of support we discussed in Chapter 13 and use them when you feel you need to.
- Do the next bit of planning – this is usually easier than writing and can help you feel more in control; it is often time invested, not wasted. It can help you take a step back, look at your overall progress and begin to move forward again.
- Break the work down into smaller parts – this is the salami method again and when things are difficult, they often seem much bigger. Breaking them down into smaller parts means they may well feel much more manageable. Make sure your goals are broken down too, so instead of writing a whole section, think about writing 500 words of it instead. You could also try using the Pomodoro technique, which involves focused work sessions with frequent short breaks and is known for promoting sustained concentration and staving off mental fatigue. Choose a particular task, set a timer for 25 minutes and work on the task until the timer goes. Then take a break for five minutes, set the timer for another 25 minutes and start again. After doing this four times, take a longer break of 15–30 minutes.
- Give yourself a reward – when you complete something, reward yourself with something you know you enjoy.
- Keep a list of things you have done – many of us know the value of a 'to-do' list but having a 'done list' can be a very good motivator too.
- Remember your passion – remind yourself why you wanted to do your study.

- Don't be too hard on yourself – many of us are our own worst critic and need to remember how far we have come.
- Try not to compare yourself with other people – there will always be people who seem further ahead than you are. Focus on yourself and what you want to achieve next.

EMMA

I've been making quite good progress with my research project but I'm starting to feel like I'm running out of steam. I've been thinking about different ways I can keep motivated and I think some rewards will help. I feel like my whole life is work at the moment, so I'm going to give myself a bit of time off. One of my friends feels the same, so we're going to see a film together and have something to eat. We've also talked about being in touch at the end of each day to say how we've been getting on and meeting up for a weekly coffee and chat.

Sometimes students say to me that they feel like giving up. At times like these they might well have experienced some setbacks that can feel like big obstacles in the way, either practical or personal. While the thought of giving up might be tempting at times, they usually feel there is too much at stake and the price is too great to pay; this thought often keeps them going.

At times like this, it will be important to process your feelings so you can deal with them. Boud et al's (1985) reflective model is useful here as it encourages us to pay attention to our feelings, so we can address them. Their model has the following three stages:

- Returning to the experience – this involves looking back on what has been happening and could include discussing it with others. This helps us to start to identify where our feelings are coming from.
- Attending to feelings – this means paying attention to the way we feel and involves two important aspects: building on the positive feelings and removing those that are negative or getting in the way.
- Re-evaluating the experience – this is the most important stage. The new knowledge we now have about our positive and negative feelings and how to deal with them is added to what we know about ourselves already, and we begin to think about things differently and take action accordingly.

Boud et al (1985) argue that if we don't process our feelings (particularly our negative feelings) and take appropriate action as a result, it is likely that they will remain. These could then become a significant barrier to our development. Processing feelings involves externalising them and this can be done in a number of ways (see Figure 14.1). Writing in a journal can help, others prefer to talk to a trusted friend or relative. If you find yourself in the position where you are seriously thinking of giving up, do speak to your supervisor or Programme Director or Course Leader as soon as you can, as there will often be a way forward even if you can't see it at the moment.

Figure 14.1: Processing negative feelings to externalise them

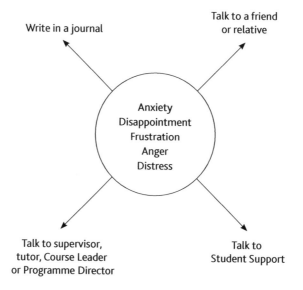

 If you genuinely feel like giving up, try writing in your research journal. Some people experience a very real sense of relief as they put their thoughts on paper, getting them out of their head, and leaving them there.

It's good to remind yourself that things that really matter are often challenging. Writing a dissertation is a case in point because of the number of credits involved and the proportion of the marks it will contribute to your overall degree classification. The vast majority of the students I work with want to do themselves justice, and something many of them don't realise is how much of themselves they are investing in their work. This includes not only their time and effort, but their emotions and their relationships too. Some will even say things like 'I've given my heart and soul to this'. I am always encouraged by this and say to them that it is good that it matters so much, because that's when we put in the effort needed and probably get a better mark as a result. Our human nature is such that if it didn't really matter, we wouldn't make as much effort, and we could then face disappointing consequences.

Some general strategies for managing stress

Completing a dissertation can be a stressful time for many students, so it is good to think about what you can do to try and remain as calm as you can. This is not always easy, especially if you suffer from anxiety like Rajesh, and how people cope with stress varies from person to person. This means that the most important thing is to find what works for you and to take some action rather than thinking you should be able to cope. However, it's also good to be aware that a particular technique might work for a while and then become less effective. At this point you may well need to change your approach and do something different. As well as effective time management and making sure you are accessing the support you need, here are some other strategies that might help:

- Doing some physical exercise – this helps because it uses up excess adrenalin and releases endorphins, our 'feel-good' hormones. It also means we have to take some time out, which distracts us from whatever is making us anxious. All exercise is good, but writing a dissertation often means we spend a lot of time looking at a computer screen indoors and so getting some fresh air can revitalise us. It doesn't really matter what kind of exercise you do, as long as you enjoy it. If it really doesn't appeal to you, think about asking a friend to join you for a brisk walk – often regarded as the best exercise we can get.
- Consider using some relaxation techniques – many of these involve breathing exercises and taking time to relax each part of your body while lying down and perhaps listening to some music that is specifically written to help. Progressive muscle relaxation (PMR) can also be helpful. This involves a sequence of steps for tightening and then relaxing groups of muscles. PMR is particularly helpful at times when stress levels are high, and because you don't need to lie down you can do it anywhere, even in the park. The National Health Service (NHS) has audio recordings available via YouTube that you can listen to, for example, via your smartphone.
- Be sure to get enough sleep – people often say that 20 minutes of relaxation equates to two hours of sleep, so all very helpful if you are finding it difficult to sleep. A simple thing like relaxing in a hot bath can also be very calming, especially before you go to bed. At this particular time of day, it's good to avoid too much activity and in particular to rest your eyes by reducing the amount of blue light they have to look at. This means taking a complete break from screens, even your smartphone! Some people now use anti-blue light glasses which can be worn at any time of day and are readily available and relatively cheap to buy.
- Make some time for yourself – this way you won't get worn down and even burnt out. Don't be afraid to take some time out to do things you enjoy. This can be a reward for sticking to your research plan and can be very motivating.
- Try to avoid unhealthy habits – this is definitely easier said than done! Spending a lot of time sitting at a computer means that we (I hope I'm not alone here!) can easily crave comfort food and other things when we are feeling stressed.

Enjoyable as they are, things like smoking, eating sugary snacks and drinking things containing caffeine or alcohol can leave us feeling worse.

- Consider trying some health remedies – there are a wide range of these on the market ranging from 'rescue remedies' to herbal teas.
- Try to think positively – remember times when you have done well in your studies and focus on these.
- Keep your eye on the end goal – your graduation is coming soon; think about how you will celebrate!

Many universities offer special activities towards the end of the academic year to help students cope with stress, so do look out for them and take part if you feel they will help you. Whether it's a yoga session, a poetry workshop or the opportunity to stroke a therapy dog, give it a try and see if it helps. There is no single or correct way to manage stress, but only a range of things to try, so find what works for you and then do more of it. Also, be willing to share your successes with those around you, as they might benefit too as well as sharing their own ideas. It's good to remember that it's very common to experience stress at a time like this and that you aren't alone. Equally, if you are too relaxed, you might be tempted not to do enough work and then not get the mark you are capable of. It's all about finding the right balance.

RAJESH

It was really good to see the person in student wellbeing again. I'd forgotten how good it is to talk things through. We were able to review my strategies for managing my anxiety levels and I realised that I'd been forgetting some of the basics that have regularly helped me in the past. I've still been listening to some music, but only during breaks for meals. I also feel I'm spending all my time inside at the moment and I'd like to get some more fresh air and exercise. I've agreed that I'll get out for a walk each day and will listen to music through headphones as I walk to help reduce my anxiety levels. I'm going to do this for a minimum of half an hour per day and ask my close friends to check in with me regularly to see how I'm getting on. This was only a few days ago now and already it's making a difference.

Graduation day!

For me, graduation day is always the best day of the year as I see the students I have worked with deservedly succeeding. Graduation day has arrived for our three case study students and all have decided to attend. Rajesh has brought his family along, Sam's mum is there and Emma's friends and partner. Everyone is proud of their achievements and are looking forward to what they are going to do next. Rajesh has a place on the master's degree he was interested in, and will be starting in the next academic year. Emma is going to start volunteering with a charity that helps offenders before deciding what she wants to do after that and Sam is taking a year out to travel and to visit some refugee camps as a volunteer before deciding on the next step. Everyone feels that the hard work has been worth it. On the day they all enjoy celebrating and are thankful for the support they have had from those around them.

Sam, Emma and Rajesh all enjoyed doing their dissertations. Rajesh feels he has learned a lot about independent learning and knows that this will help him during his master's programme. Emma has become even more interested in working with offenders and has already discussed her dissertation with people in the charity where she will be volunteering and expects to talk about her research at future job interviews. Sam is looking forward to hearing the stories of refugees first-hand during the time in the refugee camps that will be coming up soon and feels confident about engaging with refugees with empathy and understanding.

 Now, imagine you're at the end of your degree course. What would you like to take away as positives from the experience of doing your dissertation? What things might you have proved to yourself, assuming all goes well?

SUMMARY

In this chapter we have considered many aspects of managing a research project successfully. Managing it yourself is the key in many respects; careful planning and keeping a focus will help to maintain your levels of motivation. Doing desk-based qualitative research is a good option for many students, especially those who are interested in areas where it is difficult to speak to participants directly. With so many good resources available via the internet, it can offer you a great opportunity to delve more deeply into something you are really interested in. Good luck and all the very best with your studies!

Further reading

- Cottrell (2014) takes you through the process of writing a dissertation in a practical way.
- Greetham (2019) gives a thorough and detailed discussion of each aspect of writing a dissertation.

References

Abimbola, S., Molemodile, S.K., Okonkwo, O.A., Negin, J., Jan, S. and Martiniuk, A.L. (2016) '"The government cannot do it all alone": realist analysis of the minutes of community health committee meetings in Nigeria', *Health Policy and Planning*, 31(3): 332–45.

Adams, C.A. and Harte, G. (1998) 'The changing portrayal of the employment of women in British banks' and retail companies' annual reports', *Accounting Organizations and Society*, 23(8): 781–812.

Adams, J., Hayes, J. and Hopson, B. (1976) *Transition: Understanding and Managing Personal Change*, London: Martin Robertson.

Adams St. Pierre, E. 'Writing as a method of nomadic enquiry' in Richardson, L. and Adams St. Pierre, E. (2005) 'Writing: a method of enquiry' in N.K. Denzin and Y.S. Lincoln (eds) *The Sage Handbook of Qualitative Research* (3rd edn), Thousand Oaks, CA: Sage, pp 1410–44.

The Advertising Archives (nd) *The Advertising Archives*, available from https://www.advertisingarchives.co.uk/en/page/show_home_page.html (accessed 26 May 2020).

Allen, D. (2015) *Getting Things Done: The Art of Stress-Free Productivity*, London: Piatkus.

Aveyard, H. (2019) *Doing a Literature Review in Health and Social Care* (4th edn), London: Open University Press.

Aveyard, H., Payne, S. and Preston, N. (2016) *A Postgraduates' Guide to Doing a Literature Review in Health and Social Care*, Maidenhead: Open University Press.

Bachman, R. and Schutt, R.K. (2008) *Fundamentals of Research in Criminology and Criminal Justice*, Thousand Oaks, CA: Sage.

Bassot, B. (2020a) *The Research Journal*, Bristol: Policy Press.

Bassot, B. (2020b) *The Reflective Journal*, London: Red Globe.

Beauchamp, T.L. and Childress, J.F. (2019) *Principles of Biomedical Ethics* (8th edn), Oxford: Oxford University Press.

Becker, L. (2015) *Writing Successful Reports and Dissertations*, London: Sage.

Bell, J. and Waters, S. (2018) *Doing Your Research Project: A Guide for First-time Researchers* (7th edn), London: Open University Press.

Berne, E. (1961) *Transactional Analysis in Psychotherapy*, New York, NY: Grove Press Inc.

Biggam, J. (2018) *Succeeding with Your Master's Dissertation: A Step by Step Guide* (4th edn), London: Open University Press.

Blaxter, I., Hughes, C. and Tight, M. (2001) *How to Research* (2nd edn), Maidenhead: Open University Press.

Bliss, E.C. (2018) *Doing It Now: A 12 Step Program for Curing Procrastination and Achieving Your Goals*, New York, NY: Charles Scribner's Sons.

Bolton, G. and Delderfield, R. (2018) *Reflective Practice*, London: Sage.

Bonde, L.O. and Theorell, T. (eds) (2018) *Music and Public Health: A Nordic Perspective*, Cham, Switzerland: Springer.

Boud, D., Keogh, R. and Walker, D. (1985) *Reflection: Turning Experience into Learning*, London: RoutledgeFalmer.

Bowen, G.A. (2009) 'Document analysis as a qualitative research method', *Qualitative Research Journal*, 9(2): 27–40.

Boyd, E.M. and Fales, A.W. (1983) 'Reflective learning: key to learning from experience', *Journal of Humanistic Psychology*, 23(2): 99–117.

Bridges, W. (2004) *Transitions Making Sense of Life's Changes*, Boston, MA: Da Capo Press.

British Film Institute (2020) *Archive Resources Online*, available from https://www.bfi.org.uk/archive-collections/searching-access-collections/archive-resources-online (accessed 26 May 2020).

Bronner, S.E. (2017) *Critical Theory: A Very Short Introduction*, Oxford: Oxford University Press.

Brownlie, S. (2020) *Discourses of Memory and Refugees: Exploring Facets*, Cham, Switzerland: Palgrave Macmillan.

Bryman, A. (2016) *Social Research Methods* (5th edn), Oxford: Oxford University Press.

Buzan, T. and Buzan, H. (2010) *The Mind Map Book: Unlock Your Creativity, Boost Your Memory, Change Your Life*, Harlow: BBC Active/Pearson.

Case, S. (2018) *Youth Justice: A Critical Introduction*, Abingdon: Routledge.

Cohen, L., Manion, L. and Morrison, K. (2018) *Research Methods in Education* (8th edn), Abingdon: Routledge.

Coolican, H. (2018) *Research Methods and Statistics in Psychology* (7th edn), Abingdon: Routledge.

Cottrell, S. (2014) *Dissertations and Project Reports: A Step by Step Guide*, Basingstoke: Palgrave Macmillan.

Day, M. and Thatcher, J. (2009) '"I'm really embarrassed that you're going to read this …": reflections on using diaries in qualitative research', *Qualitative Research in Psychology*, 6(4): 249–59.

Denscombe, M. (2017) *The Good Research Guide for Small-scale Social Research Projects* (5th edn), Maidenhead: Open University Press.

Denscombe, M. (2019) *Research Proposals: A Practical Guide* (2nd edn), London: Open University Press.

Denzin, N.K. and Lincoln, Y.S. (2018) *The Sage Handbook of Qualitative Research* (5th edn), Thousand Oaks, CA: Sage.

Drucker, P. (1954) *The Practice of Management*, New York, NY: Harper & Row.

Eales-Reynolds, L.-J., Judge, B., McCreery, E. and Jones, P. (2013) *Critical Thinking Skills for Education Students* (2nd edn), London: Sage.

Eckstein, J.J. (2018) *Writing a Literature Review*, available from https://methods.sagepub.com/base/download/ReferenceEntry/the-sage-encyclopedia-of-communication-research-methods/i15707.xml (accessed 6 June 2021).

Etherington, K. (2004) *Becoming a Reflexive Researcher: Using Ourselves in Research*, London: Jessica Kingsley.

Evans, J. (2007) *Your Psychology Project: The Essential Guide*, London: Sage.

Faucher, C. (2009) 'Fear and loathing in the news: a qualitative analysis of Canadian print news coverage of youthful offending in the twentieth century', *Journal of Youth Studies*, 12(4): 439–56.

Finley, S. (2008) 'Characteristics of community-based research' in L.M. Given (ed) *Sage Encyclopedia of Qualitative Research Methods, Volumes 1 and 2*, Thousand Oaks, CA: Sage, pp 97–9.

Fitzgerald, T. (2007) 'Documents and documentary analysis: reading between the lines' in A. Briggs and M. Coleman (eds) *Research Methods in Educational Leadership and Management* (2nd edn), London: Sage, pp 278–94.

Fook, J. and Askeland, G.A. (2006) 'The "critical" in critical reflection' in S. White, J. Fook and F. Gardner (eds) *Critical Reflection in Health and Social Care*, Maidenhead: Open University Press/McGraw-Hill Education, pp 40–54.

Gibbs, G. (1998) *Learning by Doing: A Guide to Teaching and Learning Methods*, Oxford: Further Education Unit, Oxford Polytechnic.

Giglietto, F., Rossi, L. and Bennato, D. (2012) 'The open laboratory: limits and possibilities of using Facebook, Twitter, and YouTube as a research data source', *Journal of Technology in Human Services*, 30(3–4): 145–59.

Given, L.M. (2012a) 'Objectivism' in *The Sage Encyclopedia of Qualitative Research Methods*, available from https://methods.sagepub.com/base/download/ReferenceEntry/sage-encyc-qualitative-research-methods/n293.xml (accessed 5 June 2021).

Given, L.M. (2012b) 'Subjectivism' in *The Sage Encyclopedia of Qualitative Research Methods*, available from https://methods.sagepub.com/base/download/ReferenceEntry/sage-encyc-qualitative-research-methods/n437.xml (accessed 5 June 2021).

Grant, A. (2019) *Doing Excellent Social Research with Documents: Practical Examples and Guidance for Qualitative Researchers*, Abingdon: Routledge.

Greetham, B. (2019) *How to Write Your Undergraduate Dissertation* (3rd edn), London: Red Globe Press, Macmillan International Higher Education.

Greetham, B. (2021) *How to Write Your Literature Review*, London: Red Globe Press, Macmillan International Higher Education.

Hammersley, M. (2013) *What is Qualitative Research?* London: Bloomsbury.

Hammersley, M. and Atkinson, P. (2019) *Ethnography: Principles and Practice* (4th edn), Abingdon: Routledge.

Harricharan, M. and Bhopal, K. (2014) 'Using blogs in qualitative educational research: an exploration of method', *International Journal of Research & Method in Education*, 37(3): 324–43.

Harris, J. (2002) 'The correspondence method as a data-gathering technique in qualitative enquiry', *International Journal of Qualitative Methods*, 1(4): 1–9.

Hazel, N. (2018) '"Now all I care about is my future". Supporting the shift: framework for the effective resettlement of young people leaving custody', research report, Manchester: University of Salford.

Heale, R. and Twycross, A. (2015) 'Validity and reliability in quantitative studies', *Evidence-based Nursing*, 18(3): 66–7.

Hennink, M., Hutter, I. and Bailey, A. (2020) *Qualitative Research Methods* (2nd edn), London: Sage.

Hennink, M.M. and Kaiser, B.N. (2019) 'Saturation in qualitative research', available from https://methods.sagepub.com/foundations/saturation-in-qualitative-research (accessed 21 May 2021)

Hewitt-Taylor, J. (2017) *The Essential Guide to doing a Health and Social Care Literature Review*, Abingdon: Routledge.

Historic England (2020) *Find Photos*, available from https://historicengland.org.uk/images-books/photos/ (accessed 26 May 2020).

Honey, P. and Mumford, A. (2000) *The Learning Styles Helper's Guide*, Maidenhead: Peter Honey Publications.

Hookway, N. and Snee, H. (2017) 'The blogosphere' in N.G. Fielding, R.M. Lee and G. Blank (eds) *The Sage Handbook of Online Research Methods*, London: Sage, pp 91–113.

Jalonen, A. and Cilia la Corte, P. (2018) *A Practical Guide to Therapeutic Work with Asylum Seekers and Refugees*, London: Jessica Kingsley.

Johns, C. (2004) *Becoming a Reflective Practitioner* (2nd edn), Oxford: Blackwell.

Kakade, O. (2013) 'Credibility of radio programmes in the dissemination of agricultural information: a case study of Air Dharwad, Karnataka', *Journal of Humanities and Social Science*, 12(3): 18–22.

Kalaian, S.A. and Kasim, R.M. (2008) 'Research hypothesis' in P.J. Lavrakas (ed) *Encyclopaedia of Survey Research Methods, Volume 2*, Thousand Oaks, CA: Sage, pp 731–3.

Kolb, D. (1984) *Experiential Learning: Experience as the Source of Learning and Development*, Upper Saddle River, NJ: Prentice Hall.

Korstjens, I. and Moser, A. (2018) 'Trustworthiness and publishing' in Part 4: Practical guidance to qualitative research in *European Journal of General Practice*, 24(1): 120–4.

Kowal, S. and O'Connell, D.C. (2014) 'Transcription as a crucial step of data analysis' in U. Flick (ed) *The Sage Handbook of Qualitative Data Analysis*, London: Sage, pp 64–78.

Kumar, S. and Cavallaro, L. (2018) 'Researcher self-care in emotionally demanding research: a proposed conceptual framework', *Qualitative Health Research*, 28(4): 648–58.

Largan, C. and Morris, T. (2019) *Qualitative Secondary Research: A Step-By-Step Guide*, London: Sage.

Layder, D. (2013) *Doing Excellent Small-Scale Research*, London: Sage.

Lester, D. (1989) 'Experience of parental loss and later suicide: data from published biographies', *Acta Psychiatrica Scandinavica*, 79(5): 450–2.

Lester, J.N., Cho, Y. and Lochmiller, C.R. (2020) 'Learning to do qualitative data analysis: a starting point', *Human Resource Development Review*, 19(1): 94–106.

Lewin, K. (1951) 'Problems of research in social psychology' in D. Cartwright (ed) *Field Theory in Social Science: Selected Theoretical Papers*, New York, NY: Harper & Row, pp 155–69.

Liu, X. (2018) 'Definition of a research topic', available from https://methods.sagepub.com/base/download/ReferenceEntry/the-sage-encyclopedia-of-communication-research-methods/i12345.xml (accessed 6 June 2021).

Luft, H. (1984) *Group Processes: An Introduction to Group Dynamics*, Mountain View, CA: Mayfield.

Mackenzie, N. and Knipe, S. (2006) 'Research dilemmas: paradigms, methods and methodology', *Issues in Educational Research*, 16(2): 1–13.

McCoombes, S. (2020) 'Developing strong research questions', available from https://www.scribbr.com/research-process/research-questions/ (accessed 28 July 2020).

McCulloch, G. and Richardson, W. (2000) *Historical Research in Educational Settings*, Buckingham: Open University Press.

Maruster, L. and Gijsenberg, M.J. (2012) *Qualitative Research Methods*, London: Sage.

Maslow, A.H. (1954) *Motivation and Personality*, New York, NY: Harper & Row.

Moule, P. (2018) *Making Sense of Research in Nursing, Health and Social Care*, London: Sage.

Mueller, P.A. and Oppenheimer, D.M. (2014) 'The pen is mightier than the keyboard: advantages of longhand over laptop note taking', *Psychological Science*, 25(6): 1159–68.

Nguyen, V.T. (2016) *Nothing Ever Dies: Vietnam and the Memory of War*, Cambridge, MA: Harvard University Press.

Nguyen, V.T. (2018) *The Displaced: Refugee Writers on Refugee Lives*, New York, NY: Abrams Press.

Noble, H. and Smith, J. (2015) 'Issues of validity and reliability in qualitative research', *Evidence-based Nursing*, 18(2): 34–5.

O'Leary, Z. (2018) *Little Quick Fix: Research Question*, London: Sage.

O'Leary, Z. (2021) *The Essential Guide to Doing Your Research Project*, London: Sage.

Oliver, P. (2010) *The Student's Guide to Research Ethics* (2nd edn), Maidenhead: Open University Press.

Pauwels, L. (2008) 'Taking and using: ethical issues of photographs for research purposes', *Visual Communication Quarterly*, 15(4): 243–57.

Pauwels, L. (2010) 'Visual sociology reframed: an analytical synthesis and discussion of visual methods in social and cultural research', *Sociological Methods and Research*, 38(4): 545–81.

Pink, D. (2009) *Drive: The Surprising Truth about What Motivates Us*, New York, NY: Riverhead Books.

Pérez Alonso, M.A. (2015) 'Metacognition and sensorimotor components underlying the process of handwriting and keyboarding and their impact on learning: an analysis from the perspective of embodied psychology', *Procedia – Social and Behavioral Sciences*, 176: 263–9.

Punch, A.F. and Oancea, A. (2014) *An Introduction to Research Methods in Education* (2nd edn), London: Sage.

Roberts, L.D. and Seaman, K. (2018) 'Good undergraduate dissertation supervision: perspectives of supervisors and dissertation coordinators', *International Journal for Academic Development*, 23(1): 28–40.

Salmons, J.E. (2019) *Little Quick Fix: Gather Your Data Online*, London: Sage.

Saunders, M.N.K., Lewis, P. and Thornhill, A. (2019) *Research Methods for Business Students* (8th edn), Harlow: Pearson.

Schön, D.A. (1983) *The Reflective Practitioner*, Aldershot: Ashgate.

Scott, J. (1990) *A Matter of Record: Documentary Source in Social Research*, Cambridge: Polity Press.

Silverman, D. (2017) *Doing Qualitative Research* (5th edn), London: Sage.

Snelson, C.L. (2016) 'Qualitative and mixed methods social media research: a review of the literature', *International Journal of Qualitative Methods*, 15(1): 1–15.

Squire, C., Davis, M., Esin, C., Andrews, M., Harrison, B., Hydén, L.-C. and Hydén, M. (2014) *What is Narrative Research?* London: Bloomsbury.

Stanley, D.J. (2008) 'Celluloid angels: a research study of nurses in feature films 1900–2007', *Journal of Advanced Nursing Original Research*, 64(1): 84–95.

Stuckey, H.L. (2014) 'The first step in data analysis: transcribing and managing qualitative research data', *Journal of Social Health and Diabetes*, 2(1): 6–8.

Tarozzi, M. (2020) *What Is Grounded Theory?* London: Bloomsbury.

Tatano Beck, C. (2021) *Introduction to Phenomenology: Focus on Methodology*, Thousand Oaks, CA: Sage.

Thomas, G. (2017) *How to Do Your Research Project: A Guide for Students in Education and Applied Social Sciences* (3rd edn), London: Sage.

Thomas, N. (2020) *Little Quick Fix: Get Your Data from Social Media*, London: Sage.

Thompson, N. (2012) *The People Solutions Sourcebook*, Basingstoke: Palgrave Macmillan.

Tight, M. (2019) *Documentary Research in the Social Sciences*, London: Sage.

Tracy, B. (2017) *Eat that Frog! 21 Great Ways to Stop Procrastination and Get More Done in Less Time* (3rd edn), Oakland, CA: Berrett-Koehler.

Tracy, S.J. (2010) 'Qualitative quality: eight "Big-Tent" criteria for excellent qualitative research', *Qualitative Inquiry*, 16(10): 837–51.

Twomey Fosnot, C. (2005) *Constructivism: Theory Perspectives and Practice* (2nd edn), New York, NY and London: Teachers College Press.

University of Bradford (nd) *Writing an Undergraduate Research Proposal: Social Science*, available from https://www.brad.ac.uk/academic-skills/media/learnerdevelopmentunit/documents/workshopresources/writingyourdissertationproposal/Writing-an-UG-R-Prop-SS-Booklet---Student.pdf (accessed 5 August 2020).

von Glasersfeld, E. (2005) 'Introduction: aspects of constructivism' in C. Twomey Fosnot (ed) *Constructivism: Theory Perspectives and Practice* (2nd edn), New York, NY and London: Teachers College Press, pp 3–7.

Vroom, V.H. (1964) *Work and Motivation*, New York, NY: John Wiley.

Walliman, N. (2014) *Your Undergraduate Dissertation: The Essential Guide for Success*, London: Sage.

Wayback Machine (2014) Internet archive, available from https://archive.org/web/ (accessed 25 January 2021).

Wheeler, B.L. (ed) (2018) *Music Therapy Handbook*, New York, NY: The Guilford Press.

White, P. (2017) *Developing Research Questions* (2nd edn), London: Red Globe Press.

Wiles, R. (2013) *What Are Qualitative Research Ethics?* London: Bloomsbury.

Yin, R.K. (2018) *Case Study Research and Applications: Design and Methods* (6th edn), Thousand Oaks, CA: Sage.

Index